Spelling
Skills

Grade 4

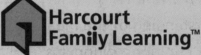

© 2005 by Flash Kids
Adapted from *Steck-Vaughn Spelling: Linking Words to Meaning, Level 4*
by John R. Pescosolido
© 2002 by Harcourt Achieve
Licensed under special arrangement with Harcourt Achieve.

ISBN: 978-1-4114-0385-7

Please submit all inquiries to FlashKids@bn.com

Manufactured in Canada

Lot #:
23 25 27 28 26 24 22
07/16

Flash Kids
A Division of Barnes & Noble
122 Fifth Avenue
New York, NY 10011

Dear Parent,

As your child learns to read and write, he or she is bound to discover that the English language contains very many words, and that no single set of rules is used to spell all of these words. This can feel rather confusing and overwhelming for a young reader. But by completing the fun, straightforward activities in this workbook, your child will practice spelling the words that he or she is most likely to encounter in both classroom and everyday reading. To make the path to proper spelling even easier, each lesson presents fourth-grade words in lists grouped by vowel sound, suffix, or related forms, like plurals and contractions. This order will clearly show your child the different ways that similar sounds can be spelled.

Each of the 30 lessons begins by asking your child to say each word in the word list. This exercise helps him or her to make the connection between a word's appearance and what it sounds like. Next, he or she will sort the words, which teaches the relationship between a sound and its spelling patterns. Your child will then encounter a variety of activities that will strengthen his or her understanding of the meaning and use of each word. These include recognizing definitions, synonyms, and base words, completing analogies, as well as using capitalization and punctuation. Be sure to have a children's or adult dictionary available, which your child will need to use for some of the exercises. Each lesson also features a short passage containing spelling and grammar mistakes that your child will proofread and correct, using the proofreading marks on page 7. Once he or she can recognize both correct and incorrect spellings, your child is ready for the next lesson!

Throughout this workbook are brief unit reviews to help reinforce knowledge of the words that have been learned in the lessons. Your child can use the answer key to check his or her work in the lessons and reviews.

Also, take advantage of everyday opportunities to improve spelling skills. By asking your child to read stories or newspaper articles to you at home, or billboards and signs while traveling, you are showing your child how often he or she will encounter these words. You can also give your child extra practice in writing these correct spellings by having him or her write a shopping list or note to a family member.

Since learning to spell can be frustrating, your child may wish to use one or more of the spelling strategies on page 6 when he or she finds a word or group of words difficult to master. You can also encourage your child to use the following study steps to learn a word:

1. Say the word. What consonant sounds do you hear? What vowel sounds do you hear? How many syllables do you hear?

2. Look at the letters in the word. Think about how each sound is spelled. Find any spelling patterns or parts that you know. Close your eyes. Picture the word in your mind.

3. Spell the word aloud.

4. Write the word. Say each letter as you write it.

5. Check the spelling. If you did not spell the word correctly, use the study steps again.

With help from you and this workbook, your child is well on the way to excellent skills in spelling, reading, and writing!

table of contents

spelling strategies

What can you do when you aren't sure how to spell a word?

Say the word aloud. Make sure you say it correctly. Listen to the sounds in the word. Think about letters and patterns that might spell the sounds.

Look in the Spelling Table on page 141 to find common spellings for sounds in the word.

Think about related words. They may help you spell the word you're not sure of.

discover—cover

Guess the spelling of the word and check it in a dictionary.

Write the word in different ways. Compare the spellings and choose the one that looks correct.

trale (trail) treighl treal

Think about any spelling rules you know that can help you spell the word.

When a singular word ends in s, ch, sh, or x, -es is added to form the plural.

Listen for a common word part, such as a prefix, suffix, or ending.

careful beginning

Break the word into syllables and think about how each syllable might be spelled.

Sat-ur-day
sur-prise

Create a memory clue to help you remember the spelling of the word.

I hear with my ear

Proofreading Marks

Mark	Meaning	Example
◯	spell correctly	I ⬭liek⬭ dogs.
⊙	add period	They are my favorite kind of pet⊙
?	add question mark	What kind of pet do you have?
≡	capitalize	My dog's name is scooter. ≡
∧	add	Scooter has ∧ spots. *brown*
ℓ	take out	He likes to ~~to~~ run and play.
¶	indent paragraph	¶I love my dog, Scooter. He is the best pet I have ever had. Every morning he wakes me up with a bark. Every night he sleeps with me.
⌄⌄	add quotation marks	⌄You are my best friend,⌄ I tell him.

Words with Short a

past	stamp	happen	grass	glad
match	magic	answer	aunt	branch
ask	pass	travel	began	half
snack	~~laugh~~	plastic	crack	banana

Say and Listen

Say each spelling word. Listen for the short a sound.

stamp

U.S. Postal Service
We're serious about mail!

Think and Sort

Look at the letters in each word. Think about how short a is spelled. Spell each word aloud.

Short a can be shown as /ă/. How many spelling patterns for /ă/ do you see?

1. Write the **eighteen** spelling words that have the a pattern, like *glad*.

2. Write the **two** spelling words that have the *au* pattern, like *laugh*.

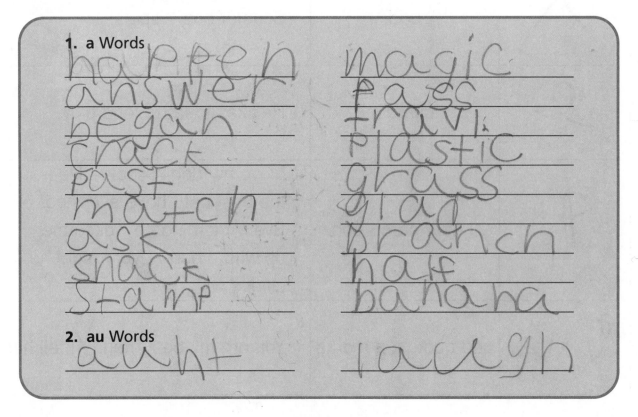

1. a Words

happen   magic
answer   pass
began   travl
crack   plastic
past   grass
match   glad
ask   branch
snack   half
stamp   banana

2. au Words

aunt   laugh

Definitions

Write the spelling word for each definition.
Use a dictionary if you need to.

1. a sharp snapping sound _crack_
2. to come to pass _happen_
3. special effects and tricks _magic_
4. to go from place to place _travel_
5. to set a foot down loudly _stamp_
6. green plants that people mow _grass_
7. a substance made from chemicals _plastic_

Analogies

An analogy states that two words go together in the
same way as two others. Write the spelling word that
completes each analogy.

8. *Opened* is to *closed* as _began_ is to *ended*.
9. *Bad* is to *good* as *sad* is to _glad_.
10. *Three* is to *six* as _half_ is to *whole*.
11. *Spin* is to *twirl* as *reply* is to _answer_
12. *Large* is to *small* as *feast* is to _snack_.
13. *Vegetable* is to *spinach* as *fruit* is to _banana_
14. *Arm* is to *body* as _branch_ is to *tree*.
15. *Black* is to *white* as *cry* is to _laugh_.
16. *Male* is to *female* as *uncle* is to _aunt_.
17. *Tomorrow* is to *yesterday* as *future* is to _past_.
18. *Question* is to _ask_ as *tell* is to *answer*.
19. *New* is to *old* as *fail* is to _pass_

past	stamp	happen	grass	glad
match	magic	answer	aunt	branch
ask	pass	travel	began	half
snack	laugh	plastic	crack	banana

Proofreading

Proofread the news article below. Use proofreading marks to correct five spelling mistakes, three punctuation mistakes, and two missing words. See the chart on page 7 to learn how to use the proofreading marks.

Proofreading Marks

◯ spell correctly

⊙ add period

‸ add

Monroe School Monthly

Weather Safety

When you are outside, be aware of the weather.

Watch ‸the sky and listen for thunder If you hear loud

crak, find shelter right away. A storm can travl fast.

To be safe, never take shelter under

a tree bransh. If you hapen to be in

a boat, head for shore You will

probably be out of danger soon.

Most storms pas quickly.

Dictionary Skills

Alphabetical Order

Dictionary words are listed in alphabetical order. Words beginning with *a* come first, then words beginning with *b*, and so on. When the first letter of words is the same, the second letter is used to put the words in alphabetical order. If the first two letters are the same, the third letter is used. Write each group of words in alphabetical order.

1. laugh   glad   stamp

glad   laugh   stamp

2. plastic   magic   grass

grass   magic   plastic

3. began   banana   brick

banana   began   brick

4. aunt   ask   answer

answer   ask   aunt

5. half   have   happy

half   happy   have

6. crack   crumb   crisp

crack   crisp   crumb

Words with Long a

awake	eight	trade	afraid	trail	waist	state
chase	mistake	weight	neighbor	plane	space	shape
paid	plain	waste	taste	wait	break	

Say and Listen

Say each spelling word. Listen for the long a sound.

Think and Sort

Look at the letters in each word. Think about how long a is spelled. Spell each word aloud.

plane

Long a can be shown as /ā/. How many spelling patterns for /ā/ do you see?

1. Write the **ten** spelling words that have the a-consonant-e pattern, like *plane*.

2. Write the **six** spelling words that have the ai pattern, like *paid*.

3. Look at the word *eight*. The spelling pattern for this word is *eigh*. The g and h are silent. Write the **three** spelling words that have the *eigh* pattern.

4. Write the **one** spelling word that has the *ea* pattern.

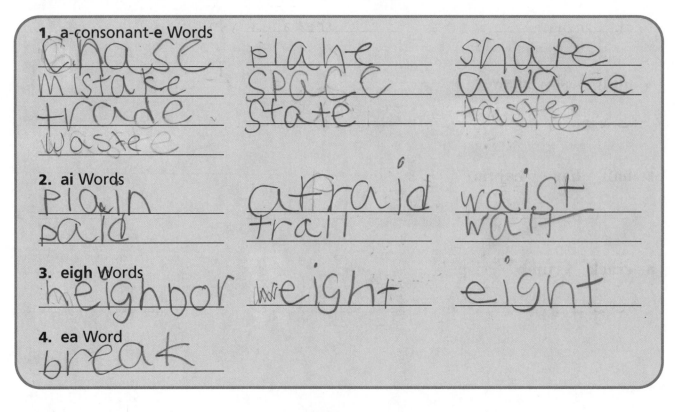

1. a-consonant-e Words

chase   plane   shape
mistake   space   awake
trade   state   taste
waste

2. ai Words

plain   afraid   waist
paid   trail   wait

3. eigh Words

neighbor   weight   eight

4. ea Word

break

Homophones

Homophones are words that sound alike but have different spellings and meanings. Complete each sentence with the correct homophone.

1. The present without a ribbon looked very _plain_ .
2. I would rather take a train than a _plane_ .
3. Don't _waste_ your time looking for the note.
4. Wear the belt around your _waist_ .
5. Alex checked his _weight_ on the scale.
6. Would you please _wait_ for me after school?

Rhymes

Write the spelling word that completes each sentence and rhymes with the underlined word.

7. I like the _taste_ of tomato <u>paste</u>.
8. Did the dog _chase_ the <u>lace</u> ribbon?
9. The boys will _trade_ the cars they <u>made</u>.
10. Rosa carried a <u>pail</u> down the _trail_ .
11. On what <u>date</u> did Florida become a _state_ ?
12. Draw a <u>face</u> in the empty _space_ .
13. Ms. Cade _paid_ for everyone's lunch.
14. What is the _shape_ of a roll of <u>tape</u>?
15. We have _eight_ pieces of <u>bait</u> left.
16. Are you ready to take a _break_ from your work?
17. It was a _mistake_ to keep the baby <u>awake</u>.
18. He was _afraid_ that he had left the bill <u>unpaid</u>.
19. I want to be _awake_ when it's time to eat the <u>steak</u>.

awake	*mistake*	*waste*	*trail*	*space*
chase	*plain*	*afraid*	*plane*	*break*
paid	*trade*	*neighbor*	*wait*	*state*
eight	*weight*	*taste*	*waist*	*shape*

Proofreading

Proofread the advertisement below. Use proofreading marks to correct five spelling mistakes, three capitalization mistakes, and two unnecessary words.

Proofreading Marks

◯ spell correctly

≡ capitalize

℁ take out

Visit Big Mountain Park

are you planning a visit to our stait?

Be sure to to stop at Big Mountain Park.

Climb the trale to Crystal Falls. Taiste the

clean mountain water. see bears and deer

along the way. Enjoy the wide open spase.

it would be be a misstake to miss this

great place!

Dictionary Skills

Using the Spelling Table

How can you find a word in a dictionary when you are not sure how to spell it? A spelling table can help you find the word. Suppose you are not sure how the long *a* sound in *neighbor* is spelled. You can use a spelling table to find the different spellings for long *a*. First, find the pronunciation symbol for long *a*. Then read the first spelling listed for /ā/, and look up *na* words in a dictionary. Look for each spelling until you find *neighbor.*

Sound	Spellings	Examples
/ā/	a a_e ai ay ea eigh ey	April, chase, plain, day, break, eight, obey

Write each of the following words, spelling the long *a* sound in dark type correctly. Use the above entry for /ā/, from the Spelling Table on page 141, and a dictionary.

1. chas   *chase*
2. awak   *awake*
3. trad   *trade*
4. ralroad   *railroad*
5. rotat   *rotate*
6. shap   *shape*
7. tral   *trail*
8. lightwat   *lightweight*
9. acquant   *acquaint*
10. betra   *betray*
11. sav   *save*

dessert
desert

Words with Short e

again	ready	heavy	breakfast	yesterday
edge	never	friend	fence	desert
bread	echo	health	stretch	sweater
ever	energy	guess	weather	against

Say and Listen

bread

Say each spelling word. Listen for the short e sound.

Think and Sort

Look at the letters in each word. Think about how short e is spelled. Spell each word aloud.

Short e can be shown as /ĕ/. How many spelling patterns for /ĕ/ do you see?

1. Write the **nine** spelling words that have the *e* pattern, like *fence*.

2. Write the **seven** spelling words that have the *ea* pattern, like *ready*.

3. Write the **two** spelling words that have the *ai* pattern, like *again*.

4. Write the **one** spelling word that has the *ie* pattern.

5. Write the **one** spelling word that has the *ue* pattern.

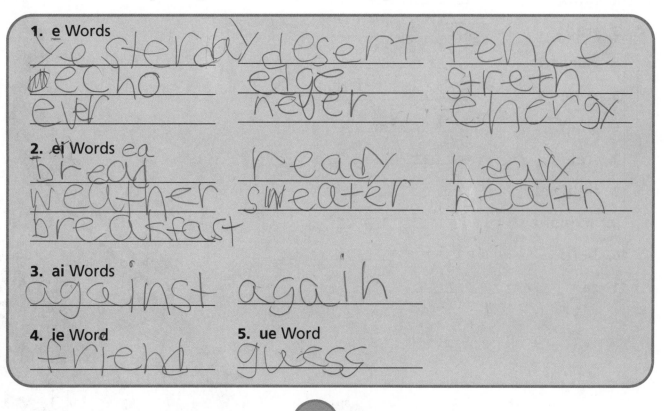

1. e Words
yesterday   desert   fence
echo   edge   streth
ever   never   energy

2. ea Words
bread   ready   heavy
weather   sweater   health
breakfast

3. ai Words
against   agaih

4. ie Word
friend

5. ue Word
guess

Antonyms

Antonyms are words that have opposite meanings.
Write the spelling word that is an antonym of each word.

1. swamp — _des_
2. sickness — _health_
3. enemy — _friend_
4. know — _guess_
5. lightweight — _heavy_
6. always — _never_
7. center — _edge_
8. for — _against_
9. tomorrow — _yesterday_
10. unprepared — _ready_

Common Phrases

Write the spelling word that completes each phrase.

11. again and _again_
12. happily _ever_ after
13. snowy _weather_
14. _bread_ and butter
15. skirt and _sweater_
16. jump over the _edge_
17. bend and _stretch_
18. the _echo_ of your voice
19. _energy_ from the sun

again	ready	heavy	breakfast	yesterday
edge	never	friend	fence	desert
bread	echo	health	stretch	sweater
ever	energy	guess	weather	against

Proofreading

Proofread the journal entry below.
Use proofreading marks to correct five
spelling mistakes, three capitalization
mistakes, and two missing words.

Proofreading Marks

◯ spell correctly
≡ capitalize
⋏ add

july 21

    Yestarday morning I played tennis my

frend Maria. The wether was hot, and we

had not eaten much brekfast. we didn't

have very much enerjy. I could hardly hit

the ball. maria couldn't run very far or

very fast.

    We will not make the same mistake

again. Next time we'll start day

with a bigger meal.

Grace
10/2/17

Guide Words

Guide words are the two words in dark type at the top of each dictionary page. The first guide word is the first entry word on the page. The second guide word is the last entry word. The other entry words on the page are arranged in alphabetical order between the guide words. When searching for a word in a dictionary, use the guide words to find the correct page.

automobile | birth

au·to·mo·bile (ô' tə mō bēl') *or* (-mō' bēl') *or* (ô' tə mə bēl') *n.* A passenger vehicle for use on land. It carries its own engine and moves on four wheels.

au·tumn (ô' təm) *n.* The season of the year between summer and winter; fall.

Ave. Abbreviation of **Avenue**.

a·void (ə void') *v.* **a·void·ed, a·void·in**...ning that blocks ...cement: *The fallen tree*
1. To keep away fro... ...urrier on the road.
prevent:

bas·ket·ball (băs' kĭt bôl') *n.* **1.** A game played by two teams. Players toss a ball through a basket defended by another team. **2.** The ball used in this game.

beach (bēch) *n.* The shore beside a body of water.

bea·con (bē' kən) *n.* A light or other type of signal that guides or warns: *The beacon guided the ship to the dock.*

beau·ti·ful ... ...di. H...

be·yond (bē ŏnd') *or* (bǐ yŏnd') *prep.* On the farther side of: *His paper route goes beyond the school.*

bin·oc·u·lars (bə nŏk' yə lərz) *or* (-bī') *n.* A device consisting of two small telescopes joined together that makes distant objects look closer and larger: *We used binoculars to see the eagle's nest.*

birth (bûrth) *n.* The beginning of existence: *the birth of the baby.*

Each pair of guide words below is followed by a list of words. Write the list words that are on the same dictionary page as the guide words.

c d e **1. after/agree**   ace   ~~again~~   ~~age~~   afraid

_____   _____

2. straight/sweet   stamp   ~~sweater~~   ~~stretch~~   switch

_____   _____

3. head/height   ~~health~~   help   hamster   ~~heavy~~

_____   _____

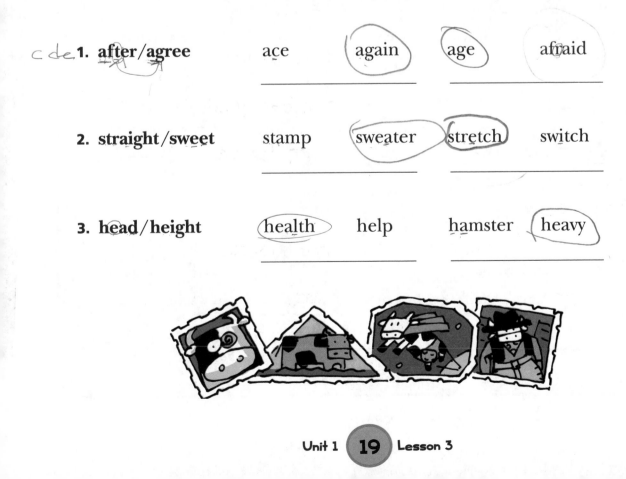

Words with Long e

season — scream — sweep — beach — means — leaf — peace
knee — reason — sweet — seem — speak — treat — please
queen — between — speech — teach — freeze — squeeze

Say and Listen

Say each spelling word. Listen for the long e sound.

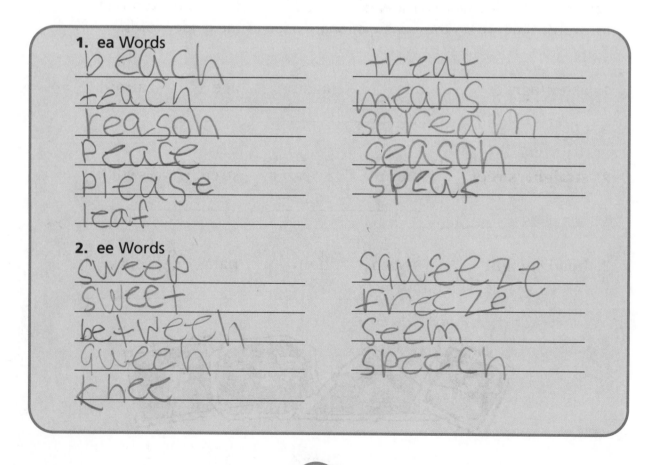

beach

Think and Sort

Look at the letters in each word. Think about how long e is spelled. Spell each word aloud.

Long e can be shown as /ē/. How many spelling patterns for /ē/ do you see?

1. Write the **eleven** spelling words that have the *ea* pattern, like *beach*.

2. Write the **nine** spelling words that have the *ee* pattern, like *sweet*.

1. ea Words

beach
teach
reason
peace
please
leaf

treat
means
scream
season
speak

2. ee Words

sweep
sweet
between
queen
knee

squeeze
freeze
seem
speech

Classifying

Write the spelling word that belongs in each group.

1. dust, vacuum, _sweep_
2. king, princess, _queen_
3. trunk, branch, _leaf_
4. ankle, thigh, _knee_
5. shout, yell, _scream_
6. among, beside, _between_
7. sour, salty, _sweet_
8. shows, intends _means_

What's the Answer?

Write the spelling word that answers each question.

9. What word do you use to politely ask for something? _please_
10. What word names a part of the year? _season_
11. What do you give a good dog? _treat_
12. What word means the same as *talk*? _speach_
13. What word means "appear to be"? _seem_
14. What do you call a public talk? _speech_
15. Where do people go to have fun in the summer sun? _beach_
16. What do you do to get juice from an orange? _squeeze_
17. What tells why something happens? _reason_
18. If a lake gets cold, what might it do? _freeze_
19. What word means the opposite of *war*? _peace_

season	reason	speech	means	treat
knee	between	beach	speak	squeeze
queen	sweep	seem	freeze	peace
scream	sweet	teach	leaf	please

Proofreading

Proofread the letter below. Use proofreading marks to correct five spelling mistakes, three punctuation mistakes, and two missing words.

Proofreading Marks

◯ spell correctly

? add question mark

∧ add

---

e-mail

New	Read	File	Delete	Search	Contacts	Check

Dear Jan,

Have you ever been a member a track team Running can really teech you what hard work meens. We run every seasen of year. It seems as if I either freaze or melt. Some days it doesn't seem worth it. Then we win, and I remember the reeson that I joined the team.

What have you been doing this spring Are you playing tennis again Let me know when you can come for a visit.

Chang

Verbs

A verb is a word that expresses action or being.

> I **ran** across the street.   Ling **is** a good writer.

Write the verb in each group of words.

1. (sweep)   girl   swan

_____

2. leaf   (neat)   seem

_____

3. team   (scream)   queen

_____

4. (between)   sweet   means

_____

5. (speak)   peace   plain

_____

6. cheese   (squeeze)   knee

_____

Months, Days, and Titles

October	Thursday	Dr.	Monday	November
February	December	August	September	Saturday
Friday	July	Sunday	Tuesday	Wednesday
March	May	June	January	April

Say and Listen

Say the spelling words. Listen to the sounds in each word.

Think and Sort

Look at the letters in each word. Spell each word aloud.

A **syllable** is a word part with one vowel sound. *Sun* has one syllable.
Sunny has two syllables: sun-ny.

An **abbreviation** is a shortened form of a word. *Mr.* is an abbreviation for *Mister.*

1. Write the **three** spelling words that have one syllable, like *March.*
2. Write the **nine** spelling words that have two syllables, like *A-pril.*
3. Write the **five** spelling words that have three syllables, like *Sep-tem-ber.*
4. Write the **two** spelling words that have four syllables, like *Jan-u-ar-y.*
5. Write the **one** spelling word that is the abbreviation of *Doctor.*

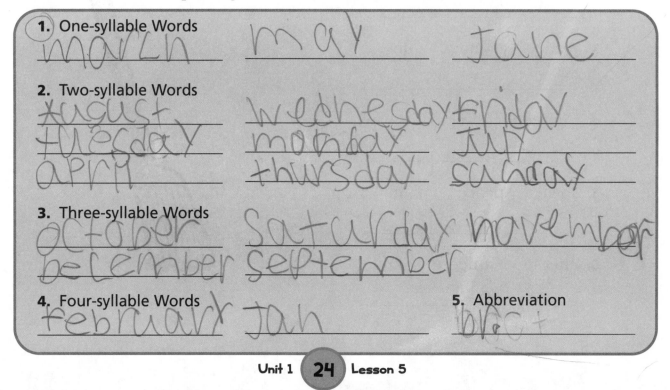

1. One-syllable Words

march   may   June

2. Two-syllable Words

August   wednesday friday
tuesday   monday   July
april   thursday   saterday

3. Three-syllable Words

october   Saturday november
December september

4. Four-syllable Words

february   Jan

5. Abbreviation

Drct

Clues

Write the spelling word for each clue.

1. the month to send valentines — *Februar*
2. the first day of the week — *Sunday*
3. the day after Monday — *Tuesday*
4. the last month of the year — *Dcember*
5. the first month of autumn — *October*
6. the first day of the weekend — *Saturday*
7. the month before December — *November*
8. the day in the middle of the week — *Wednesday*
9. the month after March — *April*
10. the first day of the school week — *monday*
11. the month after September — *October*
12. the day before Friday — *Thursday*
13. the month between July and September — *August*
14. a short way to write *Doctor* — *Dr.*

Rhymes

Write the spelling word that completes each sentence and rhymes with the underlined word or words.

15. We can play outside in *may*.
16. Will the month of *June* be here soon?
17. Kwan visited the Gateway Arch in *march*.
18. I gave Dad a new tie in *July*.
19. The new highway will be open on *Friday*.

October	Thursday	Dr.	Monday	November
February	December	August	September	Saturday
Friday	July	Sunday	Tuesday	Wednesday
March	May	June	January	April

Proofreading

Proofread the list below. Use proofreading marks to correct five spelling mistakes, three capitalization mistakes, and two unnecessary words.

Proofreading Marks

◯ spell correctly
≡ capitalize
℧ take out

Things to Do

1. call Dtr. wilson on Munday

2. bring newspapers to class on Toosday

3. go to to hockey practice on Thursday

4. turn in science report on Frieday

5. sweep driveway and take out trash on saturday

6. get present for eric's birthday party on Febuary 15

7. sign up for the the class trip in April

Dictionary Skills

Syllables

A syllable is a word or word part that has one vowel sound. If an entry word in a dictionary has more than one syllable, a dot is used to separate each syllable.

June has one syllable.

> **June** (jōōn) *n.* The sixth month of the year.

October has three syllables.

> **Oc·to·ber** (ŏk tō′ bər) *n.* The tenth month of the year.

Rewrite each word, using dots or lines to divide it into syllables. Use a dictionary if you need help.

1. January   Jan·u·ar·y
2. February   Feb·ru·ary
3. April   A·pril
4. July   Ju·ly
5. August   Aug·ust
6. September   Sep·tem·ber
7. November   No·vem·ber
8. December   De·cem·ber
9. Monday   Mon·day
10. Wednesday   wed·nes·day
11. Thursday   Thurs·day
12. Friday   Fri·day
13. Saturday   Sat·ur·day

unit 1 Review
Lessons 1-5

LESSON 1

- travel
- answer
- half
- laugh
- aunt

Words With Short a

Write the spelling word that completes each sentence.

1. I know the _answer_ to that question.
2. My dog likes to _travel_ in our van.
3. My mother's sister is my _aunt_.
4. I saved _half_ of my sandwich for later.
5. Grandpa's funny stories make me _laugh_.

LESSON 2

- mistake
- taste
- afraid
- eight
- neighbor
- break

Words with Long a

Write the spelling word for each definition.
Use a dictionary if you need to.

6. scared — _afraid_
7. the number after seven — _eight_
8. a wrong choice — _mistake_
9. the sense that recognizes flavor — _taste_
10. someone living nearby — _neighbor_
11. to split apart — _break_

LESSON 3

energy
stretch
sweater
against
friend
guess

Words with Short e

Write the spelling word that belongs in each group.

12. pal, buddy, _friend_
13. grow, lengthen, _stretch_
14. beside, toward, _against_
15. power, strength, _energy_
16. coat, jacket, _sweater_
17. think, suppose, _guess_

LESSON 4

knee
speech
reason
please

Words with Long e

Write the spelling word that completes each analogy.

18. *When* is to *time* as *why* is to _reason_.
19. *Question* is to *answer* as _please_ is to *thank you*.
20. *Elbow* is to *arm* as _knee_ is to *leg*.
21. *Notes* is to *music* as *words* is to _speech_.

LESSON 5

Dr.
Wednesday
February
January

Months, Days, and Titles

Write the spelling word that answers each question.

22. What is the first month of the new year? _January_
23. What is the shortest month? _february_
24. What day falls in the middle of the week?
wednesday
25. What is the abbreviation for *Doctor*? _Dr_

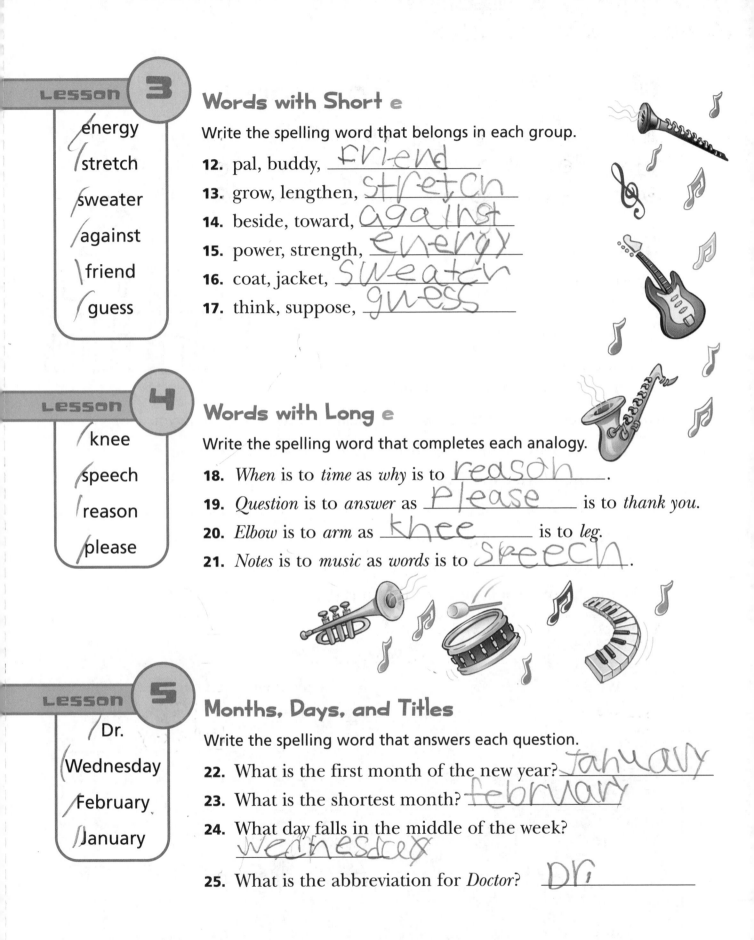

More Words with Long e

people police evening piano ski angry sorry
easy radio body copy city plenty secret
every zebra family busy pizza hungry

Say and Listen

Say each spelling word. Listen for the long e sound.

city

Think and Sort

Look at the letters in each word. Think about how the long e sound is spelled. Spell each word aloud.

Long e can be shown as /ē/. How many spelling patterns for /ē/ do you see?

1. Write the **two** spelling words that have the *e* pattern, like *zebra*.
2. Write the **eleven** spelling words that have the *y* pattern, like *city*.
3. Write the **four** spelling words that have the *i* pattern, like *ski*.
4. Write the **one** spelling word that has the *e*-consonant-*e* pattern.
5. Write the **one** spelling word that has the *eo* pattern.
6. Write the **one** spelling word that has the *i*-consonant-*e* pattern.

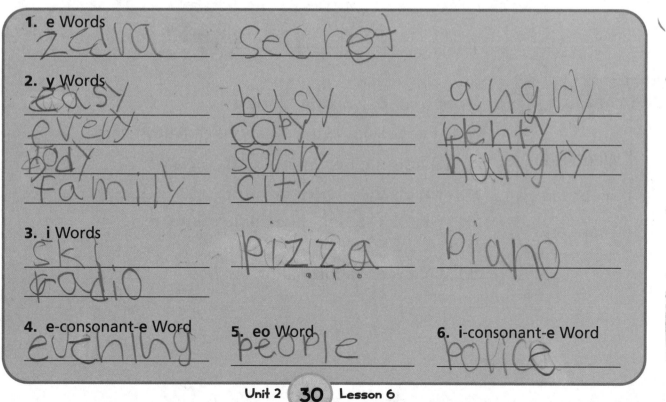

1. e Words

zebra   secret

2. y Words

easy   busy   angry
every   copy   plenty
body   sorry   hungry
family   city

3. i Words

ski   pizza   piano
radio

4. e-consonant-e Word

evening

5. eo Word

people

6. i-consonant-e Word

police

Definitions

Write the spelling word for each definition.

1. equipment used to receive sounds sent over air waves _radio_
2. something known only to oneself _secret_
3. government workers who enforce laws _police_
4. feeling sadness or pity _sorry_
5. having a lot to do _busy_
6. to glide across snow or water _ski_
7. a pie with cheese and tomato sauce _pizza_
8. a striped animal related to the horse _zebra_
9. to make exactly like another _copy_
10. a center of people and business _city_
11. the entire form of a living thing _body_

Synonyms

Synonyms are words that have the same or almost the same meaning.
Write the spelling word that is a synonym for each underlined word.

12. Our homework for tomorrow is simple. _easy_
13. The teacher gave each student a chore. _every_
14. Louis is mad about losing his cap. _angry_
15. It was a lovely night for a walk. _evening_
16. Many persons were waiting for the bus. _people_
17. We have lots of food for supper. _plenty_
18. Jose's relatives had a reunion last summer. _family_
19. I'm starving, so let's eat! _hungry_

people	radio	family	ski	plenty
easy	zebra	piano	city	hungry
every	evening	copy	pizza	sorry
police	body	busy	angry	secret

Proofreading

Proofread the ad below. Use proofreading marks to correct five spelling mistakes, three capitalization mistakes, and two unnecessary words.

Proofreading Marks

◯ spell correctly

☰ capitalize

◞ take out

Yard Sale

Family of seven is having a yard sale! It will

be held on saturday, May 7, at 333 Hilly Drive.

The house is is eazy to find. Just turn left off

Highway 3 at harvey Street. follow the signs at

evry street corner. There will be plenty

of good stuff and lots of peeple.

Come early before we we

get too bizzy!

Language Connection

Commas

A series is a list of three or more items.
Use a comma to separate the items in a series.

> Dave has a cat, a dog, and a hamster.

> On our vacation we rode in a car, flew in a plane, and sailed in a boat.

Write the sentences below, adding commas where they are needed.

1. I told the secret to Amy Will and Edward.

_____

2. I love music so much that I play the violin the piano and the flute.

_____

3. At the zoo we saw a zebra an elephant and a lion.

_____

4. I like pizza with cheese peppers and onions.

_____

5. Everyone in my family likes to ski skate and sled.

_____

6. The busy city has plenty of people cars and buses.

_____

7. Rita Jenna Karen and Kim play soccer.

_____

Words with Short i

quick	picture	written	picnic	itch
deliver	middle	bridge	inch	chicken
gym	interesting	guitar	begin	building
different	village	thick	pitch	package

Say and Listen

Say each spelling word. Listen for the short *i* sound.

Think and Sort

bridge

Look at the letters in each word. Think about how short *i* is spelled. Spell each word aloud.

Short *i* can be shown as /ĭ/. How many spelling patterns for /ĭ/ do you see?

1. Write the **two** spelling words that have the *a* pattern, like *package*.

2. Write the **one** spelling word that has the *y* pattern.

3. Write the **fifteen** spelling words that have the *i* pattern, like *pitch*.

4. Write the **two** spelling words that have the *ui* pattern, like *building*.

1. a Words

_____   _____

2. y Word

_____

3. i Words

_____   _____   _____

_____   _____   _____

_____   _____   _____

_____   _____   _____

_____   _____   _____

4. ui Words

_____   _____

Antonyms

Write the spelling word that is an antonym of each underlined word.

1. Michael wants to <u>catch</u> the baseball. _____

2. Those two pictures are <u>alike</u>. _____

3. Can we <u>finish</u> reading the story now? _____

4. Yoshi was <u>slow</u> to finish the job. _____

5. The gravy was too <u>thin</u>. _____

6. The movie about whales was very <u>boring</u>. _____

7. I couldn't read the words I had <u>erased</u>. _____

8. The store will <u>receive</u> our new furniture. _____

Classifying

Write the spelling word that belongs in each group.

9. duck, goose, _____

10. foot, yard, _____

11. tunnel, arch, _____

12. beginning, end, _____

13. photo, drawing, _____

14. city, town, _____

15. violin, banjo, _____

16. box, carton, _____

17. tickle, scratch, _____

18. making, constructing, _____

19. cafeteria, classroom, _____

quick	picture	written	picnic	itch
deliver	middle	bridge	inch	chicken
gym	interesting	guitar	begin	building
different	village	thick	pitch	package

Proofreading

Proofread the movie review below. Use proofreading marks to correct five spelling mistakes, three capitalization mistakes, and two punctuation mistakes.

Proofreading Marks

◯ spell correctly

≡ capitalize

? add question mark

Movie Review

A large thik cloud of smoke drops to the earth. The cloud settles on a bridge near a small vilige. It is the middel of the day. people drive their cars over the bridge and through the smoke. Then they disappear! Where do they go Soon the smoke cloud takes the shape of a bilding. firefighters hear

voices inside, but no one is quik enough to catch up with it. What is the smoke cloud? Will it return See the movie *Space Visitors* and find out. it's out of this world!

Dictionary Skills

Entry Words

The words listed and explained in a dictionary are called entry words. An entry word in a dictionary is divided into syllables.

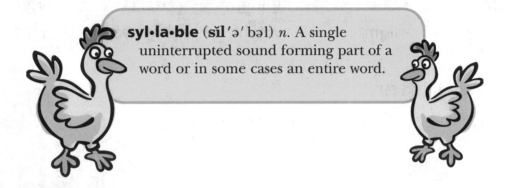

syl·la·ble (sĭl′ə′ bəl) *n.* A single uninterrupted sound forming part of a word or in some cases an entire word.

Read the examples of entry words below. Count how many syllables each word has and write the number.

1. chick•en _____

2. pitch _____

3. de•liv•er _____

Find each of the words below in a dictionary. Use dots or lines to write them in syllables.

4. guitar _____

5. picture _____

6. picnic _____

7. written _____

8. begin _____

9. package _____

10. different _____

11. building _____

Words with Long i

night	fight	die	supply	high
dry	flight	spy	lightning	deny
mighty	right	midnight	reply	bright
tie	might	tonight	highway	sight

Say and Listen

Say each spelling word. Listen for the long *i* sound.

Think and Sort

Look at the letters in each word. Think about how long *i* is spelled. Spell each word aloud.

Long *i* can be shown as /ī/. How many spelling patterns for /ī/ do you see?

lightning

1. Look at the word *night*. The spelling pattern for this word is *igh*. The *g* and *h* are silent. Write the **thirteen** spelling words that have the *igh* pattern.

2. Write the **five** spelling words that have the *y* pattern, like *deny*.

3. Write the **two** spelling words that have the *ie* pattern, like *tie*.

1. **igh** Words

_____   _____   _____
_____   _____   _____
_____   _____   _____
_____   _____   _____
_____

2. **y** Words

_____   _____   _____
_____   _____

3. **ie** Words

_____   _____

Analogies

Write the spelling word that completes each analogy.

1. *In* is to *out* as *dim* is to _____.

2. *Left* is to _____ as *up* is to *down*.

3. *Weak* is to *helpless* as *strong* is to _____.

4. *Day* is to *light* as _____ is to *dark*.

5. *Rumble* is to *thunder* as *flash* is to _____.

6. *Down* is to *low* as *up* is to _____.

7. *Ear* is to *hearing* as *eye* is to _____.

8. *Gift* is to *present* as *answer* is to _____.

9. *No* is to *yes* as _____ is to *admit*.

10. *Wet* is to _____ as *hot* is to *cold*.

Definitions

Write the spelling word for each definition. Use a dictionary if you need to.

11. the middle of the night _____

12. to make a bow or a knot _____

13. great strength _____

14. an airplane trip _____

15. to struggle _____

16. to live no more _____

17. this night _____

18. the amount available _____

19. a secret agent _____

night	fight	die	supply	high
dry	flight	spy	lightning	deny
mighty	right	midnight	reply	bright
tie	might	tonight	highway	sight

Proofreading

Proofread the invitation below. Use proofreading marks to correct five spelling mistakes, three capitalization mistakes, and two unnecessary words.

Proofreading Marks

◯ spell correctly
≡ capitalize
℘ take out

You Are Invited!

What: a a slumber party

Where: jessica Ramon's house

When: Friday, september 5

Time: 8:00 P.M. until 9:00 A.M. Saturday

Bring: a suply of your favorite games

a sleeping bag to spend the nite

a midnigt movie—a spie or mystery video

Please replie to Mrs. Ramon at 888-4999

by by august 31.

Dictionary Skills

Multiple Meanings

Many words in a dictionary have more than one meaning.
These entries for *bright* and *high* give two or three meanings.

> **bright** (brīt) *adj.* **bright·er, bright·est.**
> **1.** Giving off light in large amounts:
> *the bright sun.* **2.** Smart: *a bright child.*

> **high** (hī) *adj.* **high·er, high·est.**
> **1.** Extending far up; tall: *twenty feet high.*
> **2.** Far above the ground: *a high branch.*
> **3.** Above average: *high grades.*

Write the number of the *bright* definition that goes with each sentence.

1. My dog Baxter is very bright. _____

2. The moon is not very bright tonight. _____

3. The bright light hurt our eyes. _____

4. A bright child can solve problems quickly. _____

5. The cat's bright eyes glowed in the dark. _____

6. Following directions is always a bright idea. _____

Write the number of the *high* definition that goes with each sentence.

7. The sweater was nice, but the price was high. _____

8. The mountain is 15,000 feet high. _____

9. High diving is an Olympic event. _____

10. The car traveled at a high speed. _____

11. Three dollars is a high price for a pencil. _____

More Words with Long i

quiet	giant	smile	twice	child
buy	climb	blind	write	size
life	awhile	slide	surprise	wise
knife	sunshine	beside	behind	iron

Say and Listen

Say each spelling word. Listen for the long *i* sound.

Think and Sort

Look at the letters in each word. Think about how long *i* is spelled. Spell each word aloud.

Long *i* can be shown as /ī/. How many spelling patterns for /ī/ do you see?

giant

1. Write the **twelve** spelling words that have the *i*-consonant-*e* pattern, like *life*.

2. Write the **seven** spelling words that have the *i* pattern, like *child*.

3. Write the **one** spelling word that has the *uy* pattern.

1. i-consonant-e Words

_____ _____ _____

_____ _____ _____

_____ _____ _____

_____ _____ _____

2. i Words

_____ _____ _____

_____ _____ _____

_____

3. uy Word

_____

Definitions

Write the spelling word for each definition.

1. something that happens without warning _____

2. of great size _____

3. the light of the sun _____

4. in back of _____

5. with little or no noise _____

6. next to _____

7. a metal tool used to press wrinkled fabric _____

8. for a brief time _____

9. an instrument used for cutting _____

Rhymes

Write the spelling word that completes each sentence
and rhymes with the underlined word.

10. It's hard to _____ for a long <u>while</u>.

11. What _____ are the <u>pies</u> you baked?

12. She was so <u>nice</u> to call me _____.

13. He had a <u>wife</u> for forty years of his _____.

14. Let's _____ Dad the yellow <u>tie</u>.

15. The _____ had a <u>mild</u> cold.

16. Mike and Ike <u>tried</u> to _____ down the hill.

17. It will take a long <u>time</u> to _____ that mountain.

18. It is _____ not to tell <u>lies</u>.

19. The children were <u>kind</u> to the _____ bird.

quiet	giant	smile	twice	child
buy	climb	blind	write	size
life	awhile	slide	surprise	wise
knife	sunshine	beside	behind	iron

Proofreading

Proofread this paragraph from a report. Use proofreading marks to correct five spelling mistakes, three punctuation mistakes, and two unnecessary words.

Proofreading Marks

◯ spell correctly
⊙ add period
ℓ take out

Project1 : Raccoon Report

Raccoons in the Neighborhood

You probably have a raccoon in your liffe, no matter where you live. A raccoon is a queit, furry animal with a ringed tail It might surprize you some night by your garbage can. It is a wize animal and and can figure out how to get the lid off It looks like a robber because it has a black mask across its eyes. It may run off and clime a tree. It may also sit there looking friendly. Don't think that it will make a a good pet, though It's a wild animal.

Nouns

A noun is a word that names a person, a place, a thing, or an idea.
Look at the nouns below.

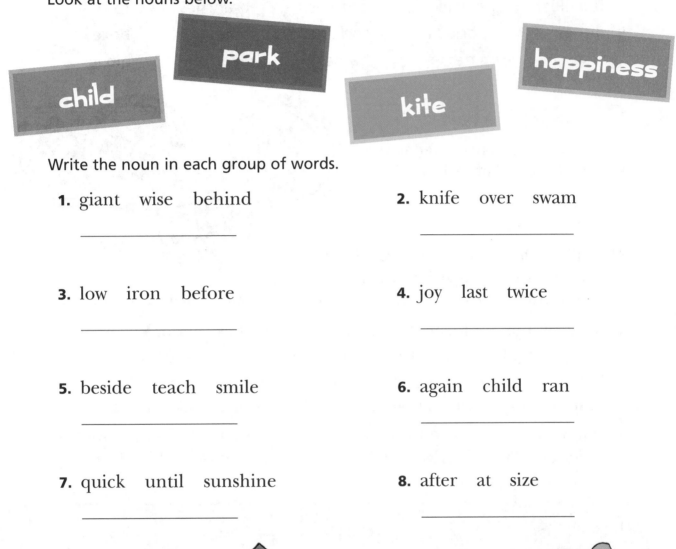

park

child

kite

happiness

Write the noun in each group of words.

1. giant   wise   behind

_____

2. knife   over   swam

_____

3. low   iron   before

_____

4. joy   last   twice

_____

5. beside   teach   smile

_____

6. again   child   ran

_____

7. quick   until   sunshine

_____

8. after   at   size

_____

Plural Words

brothers	pennies	buses	inches	stories
families	classes	brushes	branches	foxes
dishes	pockets	rocks	hikes	boxes
trees	cities	babies	peaches	gloves

Say and Listen

Say the spelling words. Listen to the sounds at the end of each word.

Think and Sort

pennies

All of the spelling words are plurals. **Plurals** are words that name more than one thing. Look at the spelling words. Think about how each plural was formed. Spell each word aloud.

1. Most plurals are formed by adding -*s* to the base word. Write the **six** spelling words that are formed by adding -*s*, like *trees*.

2. Some plurals are formed by adding -*es* to the base word. Write the **nine** spelling words that are formed by adding -*es*, like *inches*.

3. If a word ends in a consonant and *y*, the *y* is changed to *i* before -*es* is added. Write the **five** spelling words that are formed by dropping *y* and adding -*ies*, like *cities*.

1. -s Plurals

_____ _____ _____

_____ _____ _____

2. -es Plurals

_____ _____ _____

_____ _____ _____

_____ _____ _____

3. -ies Plurals

_____ _____

_____ _____

Classifying

Write the spelling word that belongs in each group.

1. planes, trains, _____
2. villages, towns, _____
3. pebbles, stones, _____
4. fathers, uncles, _____
5. dimes, nickels, _____
6. jars, cans, _____
7. yards, feet, _____
8. dogs, wolves, _____
9. leaves, twigs, _____
10. adults, children, _____
11. tales, legends, _____

What's the Answer?

Write the spelling word that answers each question.

12. What do mothers, fathers, and children belong to? _____
13. On what do apples and oranges grow? _____
14. What holds coins, wallets, and other things? _____
15. What are long walks on foot? _____
16. If it's cold, what do you wear on your hands? _____
17. On what do people serve food? _____
18. What do teachers call groups of students? _____
19. What do you use on your hair and your teeth? _____

brothers	pennies	buses	inches	stories
families	classes	brushes	branches	foxes
dishes	pockets	rocks	hikes	boxes
trees	cities	babies	peaches	gloves

Proofreading

Proofread the newspaper article below. Use proofreading marks to correct five spelling mistakes, three punctuation mistakes, and two missing words.

Proofreading Marks

◯ spell correctly

⊙ add period

∧ add

Outdoor Life

Outdoor Fun in the City

by Mark Swift

Many famillys living in citys can't take hiks in the woods They have to visit parks to enjoy nature. Many parks have trees and rockes climb. They also have wild

animals such rabbits and squirrels to watch

Many animal babyes are born in the spring. It's the perfect season for enjoying park wildlife

Subject of a Sentence

The subject of a sentence is the person or thing that is doing the action or is being talked about. To find the subject, first find the predicate. Then ask yourself who or what does the action in the predicate. The answer is the subject of the sentence. In the sentence below, *marched past the palace* is the predicate, so *The brave soldiers* is the subject of the sentence.

> **The brave soldiers** marched past the palace.

Write the subject of each sentence below.

1. Peaches grow on the tree in my grandmother's front yard.

_____

2. Her older brothers go to high school.

_____

3. Two cardboard boxes tumbled off the shelf.

_____

4. Dance classes begin at three o'clock.

_____

5. My aunt's twin babies look exactly alike.

_____

6. The oak trees lost their leaves in October.

_____

unit 2 Review
Lessons 6-10

LESSON 6

secret
family
evening
people
radio
police

More Words with Long e

Write the spelling word for each clue.

1. Your cousins, uncles, and aunts are part of this group. _____
2. This is something you should keep. _____
3. This plays music. _____
4. This time of day happens after sunset. _____
5. All men, women, and children make up this group. _____
6. These people protect our communities. _____

LESSON 7

picture
interesting
different
gym
package
building

Words with Short i

Write the spelling word for each definition.

7. a room used for playing sports _____
8. a place with offices where people work _____
9. not the same _____
10. a box or bundle containing something _____
11. holding one's attention _____
12. a photo, painting, or drawing _____

LESSON 8

lightning

tonight

supply

tie

Words with Long i

Write the spelling word that belongs in each group.

13. rain, thunder, _____

14. coat, shirt, _____

15. today, tomorrow, _____

16. give, provide, _____

LESSON 9

surprise

quiet

climb

buy

More Words with Long i

Write the spelling word that is a synonym for each underlined word or words.

17. You should be <u>silent</u> during a movie. _____

18. Eva wants to <u>purchase</u> that watch. _____

19. The two boys will <u>move up</u> the playground ladders. _____

20. Imagine my <u>amazement</u> when I saw you! _____

LESSON 10

brothers

inches

families

pennies

babies

Plural Words

Write the spelling word that completes each analogy.

21. *Ones* is to *hundreds* as _____ is to *dollars*.

22. *Does* is to *fawns* as *mothers* is to _____.

23. *Meters* is to *centimeters* as *yards* is to _____.

24. *Girls* is to *sisters* as *boys* is to _____.

25. *Dens* is to *lions* as *houses* is to _____.

Words with Short o

hobby	doctor	wallet	watch	swallow
wash	contest	cotton	knock	beyond
model	object	dollar	problem	knot
forgot	o'clock	solve	bottom	hospital

Say and Listen

Say each spelling word. Listen for the short o sound.

dollar

Think and Sort

Look at the letters in each word. Think about how short o is spelled. Spell each word aloud.

Short o can be shown as /ŏ/. How many spelling patterns for /ŏ/ do you see?

1. Write the **sixteen** spelling words that have the *o* pattern, like *solve*.
2. Write the **four** spelling words that have the *a* pattern, like *wash*.

1. o Words

_____   _____
_____   _____
_____   _____
_____   _____
_____   _____
_____   _____
_____   _____
_____   _____

2. a Words

_____   _____
_____   _____

Classifying

Write the spelling word that belongs in each group.

1. sparrow, wren, _____

2. tap, _____, bang

3. clean, scrub, _____

4. see, _____, observe

5. dime, quarter, _____

6. unscramble, answer, _____

7. _____, silk, wool

8. race, game, _____

9. goal, _____, purpose

10. billfold, _____, purse

11. example, _____, copy

12. past, over, _____

What's the Answer?

Write the spelling word that answers each question.

13. Whom do people call when they are sick? _____

14. What is the opposite of *remembered*? _____

15. What word means "of the clock"? _____

16. What can be tied in a rope or cord? _____

17. What is the opposite of *top*? _____

18. Stamp collecting is an example of what? _____

19. What comes before a solution? _____

hobby	doctor	wallet	watch	swallow
wash	contest	cotton	knock	beyond
model	object	dollar	problem	knot
forgot	o'clock	solve	bottom	hospital

Proofreading

Proofread the contest announcement below. Use proofreading marks to correct five spelling mistakes, three capitalization mistakes, and two punctuation mistakes.

Proofreading Marks

◯ spell correctly

≡ capitalize

⊙ add period

Model Plane Contest

Do you build model planes for a hobbie? enter

this contest and win a fifty-dollar prize! You can

also win a new leather walet or a cool wotch.

Fill out the form at the bottom of this page

Bring your completed form and your plane to

the school gym by ten oclock friday morning.

anyone can enter

Dictionary Skills

Parts of Speech

A dictionary lists the part of speech for each entry word. For example, a word may be a noun (*n.*) or a verb (*v.*). Most dictionaries abbreviate the part of speech. Here are some common abbreviations for the parts of speech.

> noun **n.**   adjective **adj.**   preposition **prep.**   verb **v.**   adverb **adv.**

Write the following words in alphabetical order. Look up each word in a dictionary and write its part of speech.

forgot

hospital

problem

knock

cotton   dollar   beyond

Word	Part of Speech
1. _____	_____
2. _____	_____
3. _____	_____
4. _____	_____
5. _____	_____
6. _____	_____
7. _____	_____

Words with Long o

clothes	obey	coach	only	soap
total	throat	coast	comb	zero
oak	pony	goes	motor	toe
ocean	poem	almost	hotel	program

Say and Listen

Say each spelling word. Listen for the long o sound.

pony

Think and Sort

Look at the letters in each word. Think about how long o is spelled. Spell each word aloud.

Long o can be shown as /ō/. How many spelling patterns for /ō/ do you see?

1. Write the **thirteen** spelling words that have the *o* pattern, like *zero*.

2. Write the **five** spelling words that have the *oa* pattern, like *soap*.

3. Write the **two** spelling words that have the *oe* pattern, like *goes*.

1. o Words

_____   _____   _____

_____   _____   _____

_____   _____   _____

_____   _____   _____

_____

2. oa Words

_____   _____   _____

_____   _____

3. oe Words

_____   _____

Synonyms

Write the spelling word that is a synonym for each underlined word.

1. This <u>shoreline</u> is rocky and steep. _____

2. Wally <u>nearly</u> lost the race. _____

3. You must <u>follow</u> the rules to play. _____

4. The <u>sum</u> was more than fifty dollars. _____

5. Collin <u>travels</u> everywhere by bus. _____

6. The <u>sea</u> here is very blue. _____

7. Ramon had <u>just</u> five dollars left. _____

8. What is your favorite TV <u>show</u>? _____

Clues

Write the spelling word for each clue.

9. People wash with this. _____

10. Ten minus ten equals this. _____

11. This is a place for travelers to stay. _____

12. This is a small horse. _____

13. You can use this to make your hair neat. _____

14. This can get sore when you get a cold. _____

15. This can rhyme. _____

16. This is found on your foot. _____

17. This is a kind of tree. _____

18. This person trains athletes. _____

19. People wear these. _____

clothes	obey	coach	only	soap
total	throat	coast	comb	zero
oak	pony	goes	motor	toe
ocean	poem	almost	hotel	program

Proofreading

Proofread the journal entry below. Use proofreading marks to correct five spelling mistakes, three capitalization mistakes, and two unnecessary words.

Proofreading Marks

◯ spell correctly

≡ capitalize

℘ take out

august 23

Our vacation at the coest has been so much fun.

our hotal room overlooks the ocean. Every morning

i run to to the beach for a swim. Today I stuck only

my toa in the water. It was too cold to swim. If it

doesn't warm up, Dad and I can still combe the the

beach for seashells. Our vacation is allmost

over, but it's been great.

Capital Letters

Use a capital letter to begin a person's first and last names.
Also use a capital letter to begin a title that goes with someone's name.

> **Mrs.** Emerick works in the school cafeteria.
> **Barry** and **Judy** both play sports.

The sentences below contain errors in capitalization. Write each sentence correctly.

1. laurie, amber, and keisha climbed to the top of the rope.

_____

_____

2. miss santucci said that the ropes feel as if they've been coated with soap.

_____

_____

3. On Tuesday we have basketball practice with mr. dowling.

_____

_____

4. rebecca and jamal keep track of the points that each team scores.

_____

_____

More Words with Long o

below	broke	own	shadow	slowly
elbow	though	explode	close	tomorrow
froze	knows	hollow	nose	stole
alone	pillow	chose	those	window

Say and Listen

Say each spelling word. Listen for the long o sound.

window

Think and Sort

Look at the letters in each word. Think about how long o is spelled. Spell each word aloud.

Long o can be shown as /ō/. How many spelling patterns for /ō/ do you see?

1. Write the **nine** spelling words that have the *o*-consonant-*e* pattern, like *broke*.

2. Write the **ten** spelling words that have the *ow* pattern, like *own*.

3. In the *ough* spelling pattern, the *g* and the *h* are silent. Write the **one** spelling word that has the *ough* pattern.

1. **o-consonant-e Words**

_____   _____   _____

_____   _____   _____

_____   _____   _____

2. **ow Words**

_____   _____   _____

_____   _____   _____

_____   _____   _____

_____

3. **ough Word**

_____

Antonyms

Write the spelling word that is an antonym of each underlined word.

1. The trunk of the oak tree was <u>solid</u>. _____
2. Dad <u>fixed</u> the new window. _____
3. Will you please <u>open</u> the door? _____
4. The car drove <u>quickly</u> past the house. _____
5. Aunt Cleo <u>thawed</u> the turkey. _____
6. Todd's apartment is <u>above</u> Yuri's. _____
7. Let's do the assignment <u>together</u>. _____

Analogies

Write the spelling word that completes each analogy.

8. *Eat* is to *ate* as *steal* is to _____.
9. *Board* is to *hard* as _____ is to *soft*.
10. *Leg* is to *knee* as *arm* is to _____.
11. *Sing* is to *sang* as *choose* is to _____.
12. *Yesterday* is to *past* as _____ is to *future*.
13. *Taste* is to *mouth* as *smell* is to _____.
14. *Says* is to *speaks* as _____ is to *understands*.
15. *Match* is to *burn* as *firecracker* is to _____.
16. *Dark* is to _____ as *smooth* is to *silk*.
17. *Hard* is to *difficult* as *have* is to _____.
18. *This* is to *that* as *these* is to _____.
19. *Also* is to *too* as _____ is to *however*.

More Words with Long o

below	broke	own	shadow	slowly
elbow	though	explode	close	tomorrow
froze	knows	hollow	nose	stole
alone	pillow	chose	those	window

Proofreading

Proofread this paragraph from the back cover of a book. Use proofreading marks to correct five spelling mistakes, three capitalization mistakes, and two punctuation mistakes.

Proofreading Marks

◯ spell correctly

= capitalize

? add question mark

One night Mario sat at the desk in his room. suddenly he frose. Did something move near the windoe Mario felt as thogh his heart would explode. Then he laughed. It was only his shaddow. Mario laid his head on his pillow and sloly fell asleep. then a loud knock at the front door woke him. who would be visiting at this time of night This book will keep you reading as the mystery unfolds.

Language Connection

Quotation Marks

Place quotation marks around the exact words of a speaker. Sometimes these words are at the end of a sentence. Sometimes they are at the beginning.

> Robin said, **"I'm going to the dentist tomorrow."**
>
> **"Did you hear the fireworks explode?"** asked Raoul.

Rewrite the following sentences, using quotation marks correctly.

1. Bob said, The door to the cellar froze shut.

_____

_____

2. My model car broke! yelled Michael.

_____

_____

3. Is something living in that hollow log? asked Delia.

_____

_____

4. Zak yelled, Look at your shadow on the wall!

_____

_____

5. Stay close together as we hike, said the guide.

_____

_____

6. Randi asked, Is this pillow made of feathers?

_____

_____

Words with Short u

suddenly	touch	does	tough	subject
rough	brush	fudge	country	under
knuckle	couple	hunt	until	jungle
trouble	button	enough	double	hundred

Say and Listen

Say each spelling word. Listen for the short *u* sound.

jungle

Think and Sort

Look at the letters in each word. Think about how short *u* is spelled. Spell each word aloud.

Short *u* can be shown as /ŭ/. How many spelling patterns for /ŭ/ do you see?

1. Write the **eleven** spelling words that have the *u* pattern, like *hunt*.

2. Write the **eight** spelling words that have the *ou* pattern, lie *touch*.

3. Write the **one** spelling word that has the *oe* pattern.

1. u Words

_____   _____   _____

_____   _____   _____

_____   _____   _____

_____   _____

2. ou Words

_____   _____   _____

_____   _____   _____

_____   _____

3. oe Word

_____

Hink Pinks

Hink pinks are pairs of rhyming words that have a funny meaning.
Read each meaning. Write the spelling word that completes each hink pink.

1. grooming the hair in a hurry _____ rush

2. things made out of sandpaper _____ stuff

3. person choosing the best candy _____ judge

4. something that fastens fingers together _____ buckle

5. twins who always cause problems _____ trouble

6. a piece of meat that is hard to chew _____ stuff

What's the Answer?

Write the spelling word that answers each question.

7. Where are you looking when you look below something? _____

8. Which word is a form of *do*? _____

9. What is science or math an example of? _____

10. Which word means "up to the time of"? _____

11. What is Canada? _____

12. How many pennies are in a dollar? _____

13. What can you call two things? _____

14. What is another word for *difficulty*? _____

15. To which sense do fingers belong? _____

16. Which word means "to happen without warning"? _____

17. What do you have when you have all you need? _____

18. Where might you find a monkey? _____

suddenly	touch	does	tough	subject
rough	brush	fudge	country	under
knuckle	couple	hunt	until	jungle
trouble	button	enough	double	hundred

Proofreading

Proofread the e-mail below. Use proofreading marks to correct five spelling mistakes, three capitalization mistakes, and two punctuation mistakes.

Proofreading Marks

◯ spell correctly

≡ capitalize

? add question mark

---

e-mail

Address Book	Attachment	Check Spelling	Send	Save Draft	Cancel

Libby,

    Is your oral report due next week I hope the work won't be too tuff. What is your report about I might be able to help if you need me.

    I have untill friday to prepare a rough draft of my oral report on Martin luther King, Jr. I chose dr. King because he was such a great leader of his contry.

I had no trubble finding enogh information.

Bridget

Dictionary Skills

Pronunciation

A dictionary lists the pronunciation for most entry words. A pronunciation is written with letters and special symbols. The symbols are a guide to the sounds of the word.

> **e·nough** (ĭ **nŭf′**) *adj.* Sufficient to satisfy a need: *enough money for the movie.*

Write the following words in alphabetical order. Then look up each word in a dictionary and write its pronunciation beside it.

couple   **rough**   **hundred**   **touch**

1. _____   _____

2. _____   _____

3. _____   _____

4. _____   _____

Write the spelling word that each pronunciation represents. Then check your answers in a dictionary.

5. /tŭf/ _____

6. /kŭn′ trē/ _____

7. /nŭk′ əl/ _____

8. /sŭb′ jĭkt/ _____

9. /sŭd′n lē/ _____

10. /ĭ nŭf′/ _____

Contractions

that's	doesn't	aren't	I'm	shouldn't
she'd	isn't	we're	hadn't	let's
they've	wouldn't	you'd	haven't	couldn't
weren't	wasn't	don't	didn't	they'll

Say and Listen

Say the spelling words. Listen to the ending sounds.

Think and Sort

All of the spelling words are contractions. A **contraction** is a short way to write two or more words. The words are joined, but one or more letters are left out. An apostrophe (') is used in place of the missing letters. Look at each spelling word. Think about what the second word in the contraction is. Spell each word aloud.

have + not =
would + not =
they + have =
I + am =

1. Write the **twelve** spelling words that are contractions formed with *not*, like *don't*.

2. Solve these contraction puzzles to write **eight** spelling words.

    a. I + am =   **b.** that + is =   **c.** we + are =   **d.** let + us =

    e. they + have =   **f.** you + would =   **g.** she + had =   **h.** they + will =

1. Contractions with not

_____   _____   _____

_____   _____   _____

_____   _____   _____

_____   _____   _____

2. Other Contractions

a. _____   **b.** _____   **c.** _____

d. _____   **e.** _____   **f.** _____

g. _____   **h.** _____

Rhymes

Write the spelling word that completes each sentence and rhymes with the underlined word.

1. When the bells <u>chime</u>, _____ going home.

2. The team made a <u>save</u>, and now _____ won!

3. She said that _____ <u>need</u> your help.

4. Soon _____ going to move <u>near</u> you.

5. Maybe _____ like to eat Chinese <u>food</u>.

6. After the sun <u>sets</u>, _____ take a walk.

7. Tomorrow _____ pick up the <u>mail</u>.

8. I guess _____ the last of the <u>hats</u>.

9. They _____ going to eat <u>burnt</u> toast.

Trading Places

Write the spelling word that can take the place of the underlined words in each sentence.

10. Wanda <u>did not</u> plan a fancy party.   _____

11. We <u>do not</u> want to argue.   _____

12. This pen <u>does not</u> leak.   _____

13. The bus <u>was not</u> on time today.   _____

14. The students <u>have not</u> eaten lunch yet.   _____

15. I <u>would not</u> try to trick you.   _____

16. You <u>should not</u> forget to brush your teeth.   _____

17. Broccoli <u>is not</u> my favorite vegetable.   _____

18. My parents <u>are not</u> able to go to the meeting.   _____

19. We <u>had not</u> seen the new baby before today.   _____

that's	doesn't	aren't	I'm	shouldn't
she'd	isn't	we're	hadn't	let's
they've	wouldn't	you'd	haven't	couldn't
weren't	wasn't	don't	didn't	they'll

Proofreading

Proofread this paragraph from a tall tale about Pecos Bill. Use proofreading marks to correct five spelling mistakes, three capitalization mistakes, and two punctuation mistakes.

Proofreading Marks

◯ spell correctly

≡ capitalize

⊙ add period

Pecos Bill Gets Hungry

One day Pecos Bill awoke from a long nap He'd

been asleep for ten years! he was hungry, but he

did'nt have anything to eat. He culdnn't lasso a

bull, because he had lost his lasso. He'd have eaten

snakes, but there werent' any

"I know what I'll do," bill said. "Im going to boil

my boots. i will make boot stew!" And tha'ts

exactly what he did.

Adjectives

An adjective describes a noun or a pronoun by telling which one, what kind, or how many.

> Wouldn't you like a **tall** glass of **cold** lemonade?

> The **large glass** pitcher shouldn't ever break.

Write each sentence below, correcting each misspelled word. Then circle the adjective in each sentence.

1. The video store did'nt have the movie I wanted.

_____

2. Wer'e starting a computer club at school.

_____

3. Becca dosen't want the lead role in the play.

_____

4. Yo'ud better pack your long raincoat.

_____

5. The guide said shed meet us by the iron gate.

_____

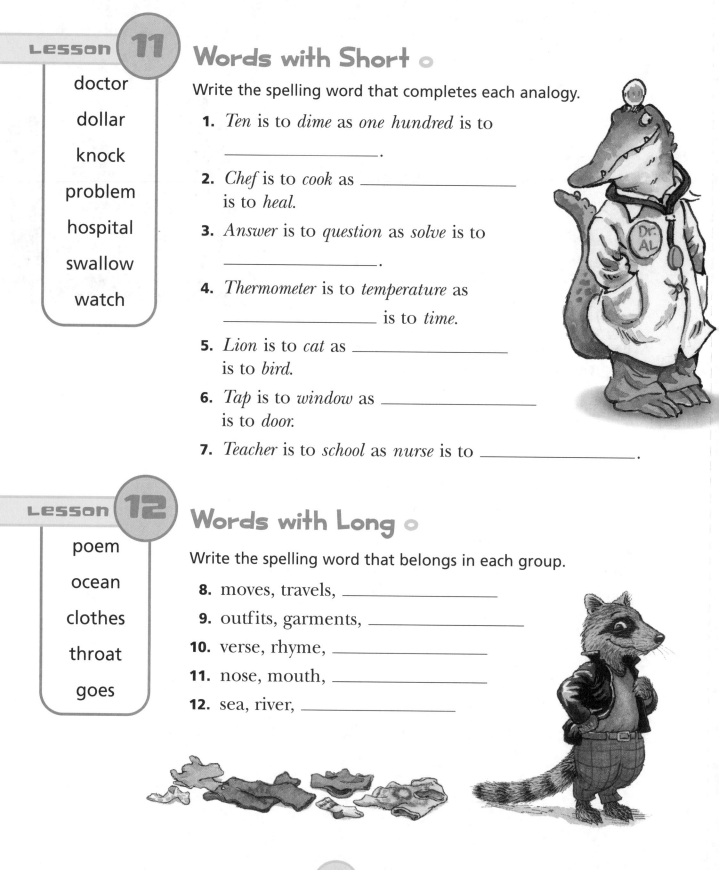

LESSON 11

doctor

dollar

knock

problem

hospital

swallow

watch

Words with Short o

Write the spelling word that completes each analogy.

1. *Ten* is to *dime* as *one hundred* is to
_____.

2. *Chef* is to *cook* as _____
is to *heal*.

3. *Answer* is to *question* as *solve* is to
_____.

4. *Thermometer* is to *temperature* as
_____ is to *time*.

5. *Lion* is to *cat* as _____
is to *bird*.

6. *Tap* is to *window* as _____
is to *door*.

7. *Teacher* is to *school* as *nurse* is to _____.

LESSON 12

poem

ocean

clothes

throat

goes

Words with Long o

Write the spelling word that belongs in each group.

8. moves, travels, _____

9. outfits, garments, _____

10. verse, rhyme, _____

11. nose, mouth, _____

12. sea, river, _____

froze

knows

tomorrow

though

More Words with Long o

Write the spelling word for each clue.

13. If something got very cold, it did this. _____

14. This word sounds like *crow*. _____

15. This word means the same as *understands*.

_____

16. This is the day after today. _____

jungle

suddenly

tough

trouble

does

Words with Short u

Write the spelling word for each definition.

17. without warning _____

18. strong _____

19. causes to happen _____

20. land with thick tropical plants _____

21. difficulty _____

weren't

doesn't

we're

they've

Contractions

Write the spelling word that completes each sentence.

22. Marco _____ have enough money.

23. I know _____ going to be late.

24. I think _____ all gone home.

25. Why _____ we warned about the storm?

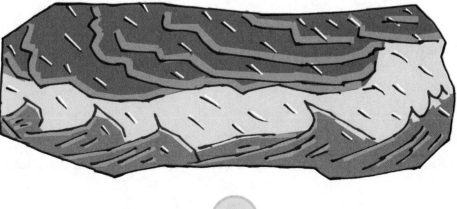

More Words with Short u

wonderful	front	cover	sponge	once
discover	other	month	nothing	become
among	brother	monkey	above	another
blood	money	done	stomach	won

Say and Listen

Say each spelling word. Listen for the short *u* sound.

Think and Sort

monkey

Look at the letters in each word. Think about how short *u* is spelled. Spell each word aloud.

Short *u* can be shown as /ŭ/. How many spelling patterns for /ŭ/ do you see?

1. Write the **sixteen** spelling words that have the *o* pattern, like *front*.

2. Write the **three** spelling words that have the *o*-consonant-*e* pattern, like *become*.

3. Write the **one** spelling word that has the *oo* pattern.

1. **o** Words

_____   _____   _____
_____   _____   _____
_____   _____   _____
_____   _____   _____
_____   _____   _____
_____

2. **o**-consonant-**e** Words

_____   _____   _____

3. **oo** Word

_____

Antonyms

Write the spelling word that is an antonym of each word below.

1. below   _____

2. back   _____

3. unfinished   _____

4. lost   _____

5. horrible   _____

6. something   _____

Clues

Write the spelling word for each clue.

7. A girl is a sister, and a boy is this.   _____

8. Food is digested in this body part.   _____

9. This is one less than twice.   _____

10. This word means "to grow to be."   _____

11. Your heart pumps this through your body.   _____

12. This can soak up water.   _____

13. February is the shortest one.   _____

14. This word means "in the company of."   _____

15. This is a chimpanzee's cousin.   _____

16. This word completes the phrase
"some ____ time."   _____

17. People use this to buy things.   _____

18. This means "one more."   _____

19. Do this to hide something.   _____

wonderful	*front*	*cover*	*sponge*	*once*
discover	*other*	*month*	*nothing*	*become*
among	*brother*	*monkey*	*above*	*another*
blood	*money*	*done*	*stomach*	*won*

Proofreading

Proofread the e-mail message below. Use proofreading marks to correct five spelling mistakes, three punctuation mistakes, and two unnecessary words.

Proofreading Marks

◯ spell correctly

⊙ add period

℺ take out

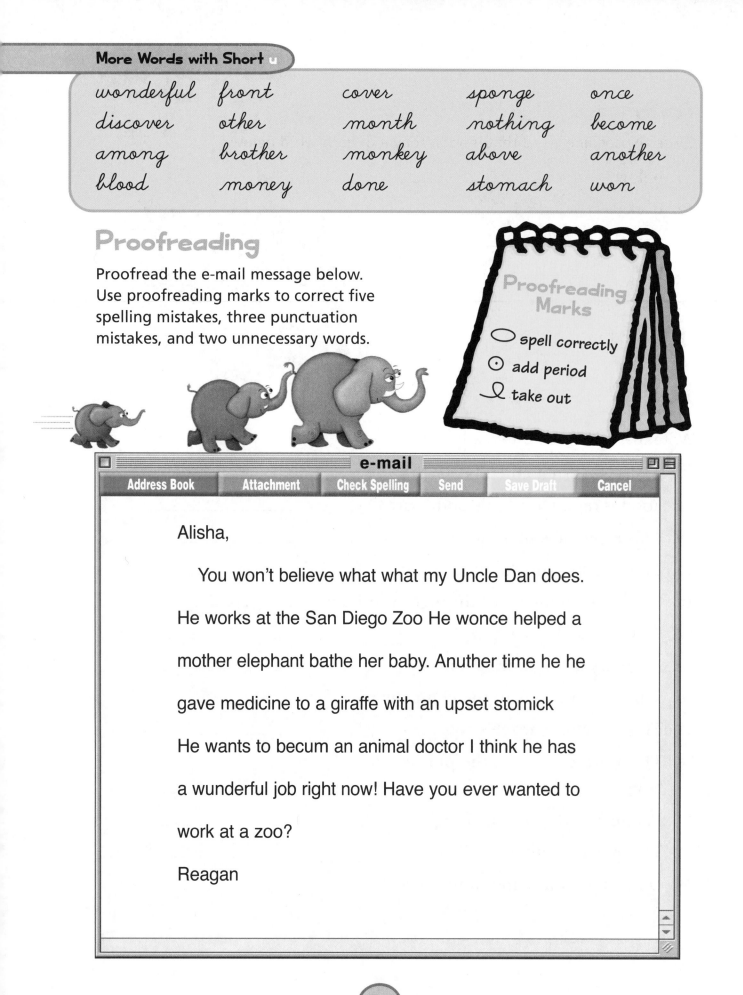

---

e-mail

| Address Book | Attachment | Check Spelling | Send | Save Draft | Cancel |

Alisha,

You won't believe what what my Uncle Dan does.

He works at the San Diego Zoo He wonce helped a

mother elephant bathe her baby. Anuther time he he

gave medicine to a giraffe with an upset stomick

He wants to becum an animal doctor I think he has

a wunderful job right now! Have you ever wanted to

work at a zoo?

Reagan

Dictionary Skills

Accented Syllables

A dictionary entry for a word usually shows how the word is said. The way a word is said is called its pronunciation. An accent mark (′) tells which syllable is spoken with more stress, or force. In some dictionaries, dark type also indicates the accented syllable.

Study the accent marks in each pair of pronunciations below. Underline the pronunciation that shows the accent mark on the correct syllable. Then write the spelling word.

1. /mŭn ē′/   /**mŭn**′ ē/   _____

2. /nŭth **ing**′/   /**nŭth**′ ĭng/   _____

3. /**brŭ***th*′ ər/   /brŭ*th* ər′/   _____

Some words have two accented syllables. The strongest accent is the primary accent: (′). The weaker accent is the secondary accent: (′).

Look at this pronunciation: /**yĕs**′ tər dā ′/.

4. Write the syllable with the primary accent.   _____

5. Write the syllable with the secondary accent.   _____

6. Write the word correctly.   _____

Look at this pronunciation: /ăf ′ tər **nōōn**′/

7. Write the syllable with the primary accent.   _____

8. Write the syllable with the secondary accent.   _____

9. Write the word correctly.   _____

Words with /o͝o/

wool	stood	brook	good-bye	pudding
understood	full	could	pull	yours
cooked	notebook	sugar	wolf	during
should	bush	wooden	would	woman

Say and Listen

Say each spelling word. Listen for the vowel sound you hear in *wool*.

Think and Sort

Look at the letters in each word. Think about how the vowel sound in *wool* is spelled. Spell each word aloud.

The vowel sound in *wool* can be shown as /o͝o/. How many spelling patterns for /o͝o/ do you see?

1. Write the **eight** spelling words that have the *oo* pattern, like *wool*.

2. Write the **six** spelling words that have the *u* pattern, like *full*.

3. Write the **four** spelling words that have the *ou* pattern, like *could*.

4. Write the **two** spelling words that have the *o* pattern, like *wolf*.

wolf

1. oo Words

_____ _____ _____

_____ _____ _____

_____ _____

2. u Words

_____ _____ _____

_____ _____ _____

3. ou Words

_____ _____ _____

_____

4. o Words

_____ _____

Synonyms

Write the spelling word that is a synonym for each word below.

1. tug _____

2. lady _____

3. while _____

4. stream _____

5. stuffed _____

6. shrub _____

If . . . Then

Write the spelling word that completes each sentence.

7. If you are cold, then put on a _____ sweater.

8. If you want dessert, then ask for cake or _____.

9. If you want to bake, then you may need _____ and flour.

10. If the meat is burnt, then it's been _____ too long.

11. If you need to write, then get a _____ and a pen.

12. If you hear a lone howl, then it might be a _____.

13. If it's not mine, then it may be _____.

14. If no one sat, then everyone _____.

15. If a bench is made from trees, then it's _____.

Rhymes

Use spelling words to complete the following poem.

16. I meant that I was able when I said, "I _____."

17. I meant that I really ought to when I said, "I _____."

18. I meant that I planned to do it when I said, "I _____."

19. I said it very clearly to be sure you _____!

Words with /oo/

wool	stood	brook	good-bye	pudding
understood	full	could	pull	yours
cooked	notebook	sugar	wolf	during
should	bush	wooden	would	woman

Proofreading

Proofread the book review paragraph below. Use proofreading marks to correct five spelling mistakes, three capitalization mistakes, and two punctuation mistakes.

Proofreading Marks

◯ spell correctly
☰ capitalize
⊙ add period

This book by Caroline lee is about her life as a young womon durring the late 1800s. on summer days she fished in a bruk on the farm In the fall she made maple suger from sap. In the spring she spun yarn from wull. She loved driving a buggy but hated churning butter. lee's book gives readers an interesting look at life in a simpler time

Language Connection

Capitalization

When the words *mother*, *father*, *mom*, and *dad* are used in place of names, they begin with a capital letter. When words such as *aunt*, *uncle*, and *doctor* are used as titles before a name, they begin with a capital letter. These words do not begin with a capital letter when they follow *a*, *an*, *the*, or a possessive word such as *my*, *your*, or *Bob's*.

> My uncle took **Mom** and **Aunt Rosa** to the doctor's office.

The following sentences have errors in capitalization and spelling. Write each sentence correctly.

1. my Father cood not fix our broken lawnmower.

_____

2. uncle frank and dad stoud in line for baseball tickets.

_____

3. Danny's Father said gud-bye to dr. dominguez.

_____

4. We took a picture of mom and dad near the wuden bridge.

_____

5. My Aunt asked uncle Mike to share his recipe for bread puding.

_____

Words with /ōō/ or /yōō/

goose	route	soup	two	new	fruit	truth
beautiful	balloon	knew	grew	cartoon	loose	choose
cougar	too	group	through	truly	shoot	

Say and Listen

Say each spelling word. Listen for the vowel sound you hear in *goose* and *beautiful*.

Think and Sort

cougar

The vowel sound in *goose* and *beautiful* can be shown as /ōō/.
In *beautiful* and some other /ōō/ words, a *y* is pronounced before the /ōō/.

Look at the letters in each word. Think about how /ōō/ or /yōō/ is spelled.
Spell each word aloud.

1. Write the **seven** spelling words that have the *oo* pattern, like *goose*.
2. Write the **three** spelling words that have the *ew* pattern, like *new*.
3. Write the **two** spelling words that have the *u* pattern, like *truth*.
4. Write the **five** spelling words that have the *ou* pattern, like *group*.
5. Write the **three** spelling words that have the *ui, o,* or *eau* pattern, like *fruit*.

1. oo Words

_____   _____   _____

_____   _____   _____

_____

2. ew Words

_____   _____   _____

3. u Words

_____   _____

4. ou Words

_____   _____   _____

_____   _____

5. ui, o, eau Words

_____   _____   _____

Homophones

Write the spelling word that is a homophone of each word below.

1. chute   _____

2. knew   _____

3. root   _____

4. threw   _____

5. two   _____

Analogies

Write the spelling word that completes each analogy.

6. *Throw* is to *threw* as *know* is to _____.

7. *One* is to _____ as *A* is to *B*.

8. *Yes* is to *no* as *ugly* is to _____.

9. *Day* is to *night* as _____ is to *lie*.

10. *Bird* is to *flock* as *member* is to _____.

11. *Dirt* is to *flowerpot* as *air* is to _____.

12. *Light* is to *dark* as *tight* is to _____.

13. *Rabbit* is to *fur* as _____ is to *feather*.

14. *Apple* is to _____ as *spinach* is to *vegetable*.

15. *Afraid* is to *frightened* as *really* is to _____.

16. *Fork* is to *spaghetti* as *spoon* is to _____.

17. *Painter* is to *painting* as *cartoonist* is to _____.

18. *Smile* is to *grin* as _____ is to *pick*.

19. *Fly* is to *flew* as *grow* is to _____.

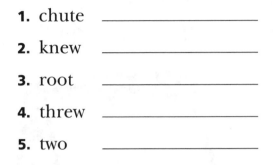

goose	balloon	group	new	loose
beautiful	too	two	cartoon	shoot
cougar	soup	grew	truly	truth
route	knew	through	fruit	choose

Proofreading

Proofread the paragraph below. Use proofreading marks to correct five spelling mistakes, three capitalization mistakes, and two punctuation mistakes.

Proofreading Marks

◯ spell correctly
≡ capitalize
⊙ add period

The Canada Goose

the name of one kind of gouse might lead you to think that it lives only in canada. The trooth is that Canada geese live throughout North America Many of these beeotiful birds live close to people. Some live in parks Others live in ponds close to neighborhoods. sometimes a groop of Canada geese chooses to make its home on a noo golf course!

Dictionary Skills

Homophones

Words that sound the same but have different spellings and meanings are called homophones. If a word is a homophone, some dictionaries list the other homophones at the end of the entry.

> **through** (thro͞o) *prep.* **1.** In one side and out the opposite side of: *through the tunnel.* **2.** Among; in the midst of: *a road through the woods. These sound alike:* **through, threw.**

Use the homophones in the boxes to the right to answer the questions and complete the sentences below. Use a dictionary if you need to.

1. Which word is the opposite of *old*? _____

2. Which word is the past tense of *know*? _____

3. Which word names a number? _____

4. Which word means "also"? _____

5. Even though the quarterback was _____,

   he _____ all the plays.

6. When the other team made _____ points,

   the star player on our team scored points, _____.

knew

new

too

two

Words with /ou/

loud	powerful	cloud	crowded	crown
counter	sour	towel	mouth	tower
somehow	crowd	ours	vowel	noun
hours	growl	south	shower	proud

Say and Listen

Say each spelling word. Listen for the vowel sound you hear in *loud*.

crown

Think and Sort

Look at the letters in each word. Think about how the vowel sound in *loud* is spelled. Spell each word aloud.

The vowel sound in *loud* can be shown as /ou/. How many spelling patterns for /ou/ do you see?

1. Write the **ten** spelling words that have the *ou* pattern, like *loud*.

2. Write the **ten** spelling words that have the *ow* pattern, like *crown*.

1. **ou** Words

_____   _____
_____   _____
_____   _____
_____   _____
_____   _____

2. **ow** Words

_____   _____
_____   _____
_____   _____
_____   _____
_____   _____

Classifying

Write the spelling word that belongs in each group.

1. robe, throne, _____
2. seconds, minutes, _____
3. eye, nose, _____
4. group, bunch, _____
5. sweet, salty, _____
6. noisy, booming, _____
7. drizzle, sprinkle, _____
8. bark, snarl, _____
9. east, north, _____
10. mighty, strong, _____
11. yours, theirs, _____
12. full, packed, _____

Partner Words

Complete each sentence by writing the spelling word that goes with the underlined word.

13. Do you want to sit in a <u>booth</u> or at the _____?
14. <u>Someone</u> somewhere must rescue the princess _____.
15. The castle had a _____ and a <u>moat</u>.
16. I'll get you a _____ and a <u>washcloth</u>.
17. <u>Rain</u> will soon fall from that dark _____.
18. Jamal was <u>pleased</u> with and _____ of his sister's work.
19. You can choose a _____ or a <u>consonant</u>.

loud	powerful	cloud	crowded	crown
counter	sour	towel	mouth	tower
somehow	crowd	ours	vowel	noun
hours	growl	south	shower	proud

Proofreading

Proofread the journal entry below. Use proofreading marks to correct five spelling mistakes, three capitalization mistakes, and two missing words.

Proofreading Marks

○ spell correctly
≡ capitalize
∧ add

october 21

I think writing amazing. a letter can stand for

a consonant or vowl. A group of letters can

form a word. The word might be a nown. At

other times it might be a verb. When words

put together in the right way, they somhow

make ideas come alive. Ideas are powrful.

i think that anyone would be prowd to be

a writer.

Language Connection

Quotation Marks

Use quotation marks around the exact words of a speaker. Capitalize the first word in the quotation.

> Chester asked, **"W**hat letter of the alphabet do you drink?**"**
> **"I** drink tea,**"** Lester replied.

Write the following sentences. Use quotation marks and capital letters where needed. Spell the misspelled words correctly.

1. Julie said, a big croud always comes to see our team play.

_____

_____

2. they practice for three howrs each day, said Brian.

_____

_____

3. even when they're behind, they don't throw in the towle, said Chris.

_____

_____

4. let's give them a lowd cheer! shouted Ben.

_____

_____

Words with -ed or -ing

swimming	changed	caused	invited	studied	saving	carrying
asked	pleased	traded	tasted	copied	cried	writing
hoping	beginning	closing	jogging	dried	trying	

Say and Listen

Say the spelling words. Listen for the -ed and -ing endings.

Think and Sort

A word from which other words are formed is called a **base word**. The spelling of some base words changes when -ed or -ing is added.

swimming

Look at the base word and the ending in each spelling word. Spell each word aloud.

1. Write the **three** spelling words that have no change to the base word, like *asked*.

2. Write the **ten** spelling words formed by dropping the final *e* before -ed or -ing is added, like *hoping*.

3. Write the **three** spelling words formed by doubling the final consonant before -ing is added, like *swimming*.

4. Write the **four** spelling words formed by changing the final *y* to *i* before -ed is added, like *studied*.

1. No Change to Base Word

_____ _____ _____

2. Final e Dropped

_____ _____ _____

_____ _____ _____

_____ _____ _____

_____

3. Final Consonant Doubled

_____ _____ _____

4. Final y Changed to i

_____ _____ _____

_____

Making Connections

Write the spelling word that goes with each person.

1. a mail carrier _____

2. a lifeguard _____

3. a runner _____

4. a cook _____

5. an author _____

6. a baby _____

7. a student _____

If . . . Then

Write the spelling word that completes each sentence.

8. If Ramon exchanged baseball cards, then he _____ them.

9. If Carlos is putting money in a bank, then he's _____ it.

10. If Amad wishes for a bicycle, then he's _____ for one.

11. If Mr. Bina is shutting the door, then he's _____ it.

12. If Tyler begged for help, then he _____ for it.

13. If Dad liked the work, then he was _____ with it.

14. If Sarah imitated the star's hairdo, then she _____ it.

15. If Troy asked his friends to a party, then he _____ them.

16. If the sun is coming up, then it is _____ to be seen.

17. If Sam wiped away his tears, then he _____ them.

18. If Lamont is not the same, then he has _____.

19. If heavy rain loosened the mud, then it _____ a mud slide.

swimming pleased closing studied cried
asked beginning invited copied trying
hoping caused tasted dried carrying
changed traded jogging saving writing

Proofreading

Proofread the magazine article below. Use proofreading marks to correct five spelling mistakes, three capitalization mistakes, and two unnecessary words.

Proofreading Marks

⟲ spell correctly
≡ capitalize
⟆ take out

Rescue Ray
by Alexa Brown

Early one morning Ray Joseph was joging down Oak street. Suddenly he heard a crying sound high in a tree. Ray wondered what could could make such a sound. Then he saw a fluffy gray kitten.

Ray studied the tree. How would he get up there? meanwhile the kitten cryed louder and louder.

Saveing the kitten was not as hard as Ray thought. Soon a little girl ran up to him. "That's my theo," she said. Ray was pleazed that he had had been able to help.

Language Connection

Predicates

The predicate of a sentence tells what the subject of the sentence is or does.

> The little girl **skipped down the street.**

Write the predicate in each sentence.

1. My cousin Jenny invited me to come to her house last summer.

_____

2. Jenny and I swam in the pool each day.

_____

3. Jenny's brothers and I traded our favorite mystery stories.

_____

A predicate often contains a main verb and a helping verb. In the sentence below, _jogging_ is the main verb. _Are_ is the helping verb. The predicate begins with the helping verb.

> My friends **are jogging down the sidewalk.**

Write the predicate in each sentence. Circle the helping verb.

4. My famous grandmother is writing a book.

_____

5. Many people are reading her other books.

_____

unit 4 Review
LESSONS 16-20

LESSON 16

discover
stomach
wonderful
once
blood

More Words with Short u

Write the spelling word that belongs in each group.

1. realize, notice, _____
2. sweat, tears, _____
3. fantastic, splendid, _____
4. lung, kidney, _____
5. never, twice, _____

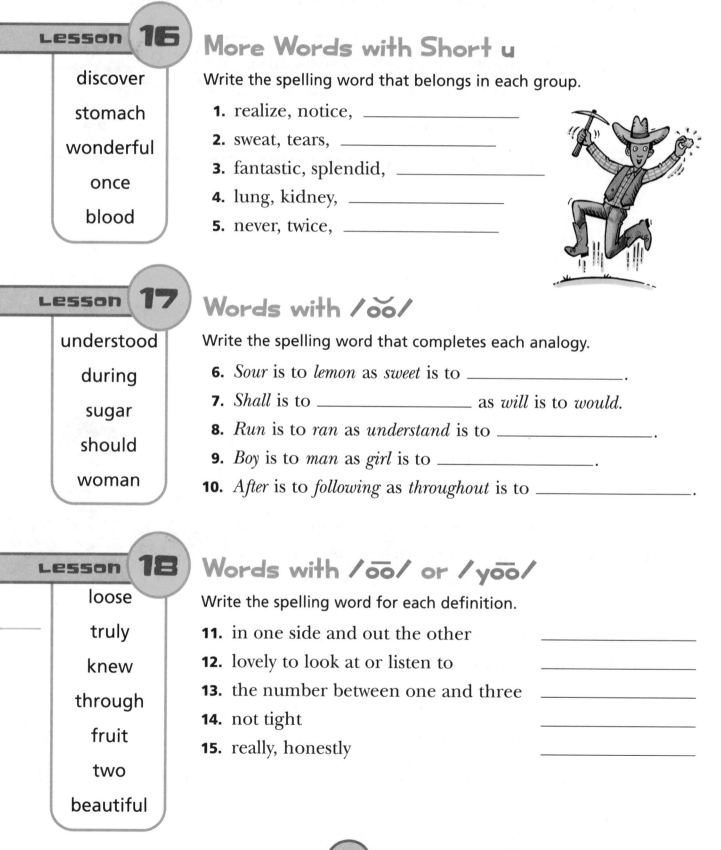

LESSON 17

understood
during
sugar
should
woman

Words with /o͝o/

Write the spelling word that completes each analogy.

6. *Sour* is to *lemon* as *sweet* is to _____.
7. *Shall* is to _____ as *will* is to *would*.
8. *Run* is to *ran* as *understand* is to _____.
9. *Boy* is to *man* as *girl* is to _____.
10. *After* is to *following* as *throughout* is to _____.

LESSON 18

loose
truly
knew
through
fruit
two
beautiful

Words with /o͞o/ or /yo͞o/

Write the spelling word for each definition.

11. in one side and out the other _____
12. lovely to look at or listen to _____
13. the number between one and three _____
14. not tight _____
15. really, honestly _____

16. the juicy, seed-bearing part of a plant _____

17. had knowledge of _____

LESSON 19

loud

ours

crowd

Words with /ou/

Write the spelling word for each clue.

18. This develops when many people gather together.

_____

19. People cover their ears because a noise is this.

_____

20. If something belongs to us, it is this. _____

LESSON 20

asked

trying

hoping

beginning

copied

Words with -ed or -ing

Write the spelling word that completes each sentence.

21. "Can you write a better ending for your story?"

_____ Elsa's teacher.

22. "I have been _____ to do that," replied Elsa.

23. "I will read the story again from the _____."

24. Elsa _____ the story for her classmates to read.

25. Everyone was _____ that the ending was happy.

Words with /oi/

coin	destroy	loyal	join	voice
moisture	employ	royal	voyage	noise
enjoy	point	poison	loyalty	soybean
spoil	employer	soil	avoid	choice

Say and Listen

Say each spelling word. Listen for the vowel sound you hear in *coin*.

royal

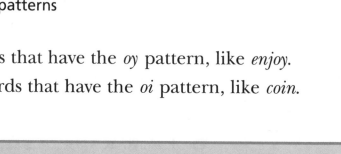

Think and Sort

Look at the letters in each word. Think about how the vowel sound in *coin* is spelled. Spell each word aloud.

The vowel sound in *coin* can be shown as /oi/. How many spelling patterns for /oi/ do you see?

1. Write the **nine** spelling words that have the *oy* pattern, like *enjoy*.

2. Write the **eleven** spelling words that have the *oi* pattern, like *coin*.

1. oy Words

_____   _____   _____

_____   _____   _____

_____   _____   _____

2. oi Words

_____   _____   _____

_____   _____   _____

_____   _____   _____

_____   _____

Clues

Write the spelling word for each clue.

1. A ship can take you on this. _____
2. This is very harmful to living things. _____
3. You can dig in this. _____
4. Dogs are this to their masters. _____
5. When you can decide between two things, you have this. _____
6. You put this in a parking meter. _____
7. The end of an arrow has this. _____
8. An opera singer uses this. _____
9. People work for this person. _____
10. This plant has nutritious seeds. _____
11. Good friends share this with each other. _____
12. Water adds this to the air. _____

Antonyms

Complete each sentence by writing the spelling word that is an antonym of the underlined word.

13. They had to _____ the old house and build a new one.
14. We can separate or _____ these two wires.
15. Will the rain improve or _____ the crops?
16. Do you dislike your dancing lessons or _____ them?
17. Hector needs silence in order to study, not _____ .
18. Will the store fire its workers and _____ new ones?
19. I will meet Laura at the store early and _____ the crowd.

coin	destroy	loyal	join	voice
moisture	employ	royal	voyage	noise
enjoy	point	poison	loyalty	soybean
spoil	employer	soil	avoid	choice

Proofreading

Proofread the letter below. Use proofreading marks to correct five spelling mistakes, three punctuation mistakes, and two unnecessary words.

Proofreading Marks

◯ spell correctly

⊙ add period

℈ take out

2840 Red Hill Avenue

Avon, OH 44011

July 17, 2003

Dear Trina,

Do you enjoi eating tomatoes? We have a great

crop this this year Too much rain can can spoyl the

crop Too little rain can destroi it, too This summer's

rains added just enough moischer to the soyle. I hope

to see you soon!

Your friend, Mark

Dictionary Skills

Parts of Speech

Some words can be used as more than one part of speech. The parts of speech include noun (*n.*), verb (*v.*), adjective (*adj.*), adverb (*adv.*), and preposition (*prep.*). Sometimes the parts of speech are listed within one dictionary entry.

> **poi·son** (poi′ zən) *n.* Any substance dangerous to life and health: *Bottles containing poison are clearly marked.* —*v.* **poi·soned, poi·son·ing.** To kill or harm with poison

At other times they are listed in two dictionary entries.

> **soil¹** (soil) *n.* The top layer of the earth's surface in which seeds are planted; dirt.

> **soil²** (soil) *v.* **soiled, soil·ing.** To make or become dirty: *Jarrell soiled his white T-shirt.*

Use *soil* and *poison* to complete the sentences below. Then write *noun* or *verb* after each to tell how it is used in the sentence.

1. Grandma planted flower seeds in the _____.

_____

2. Some everyday cleaners can _____ your plants.

_____

3. Bottles containing _____ should be clearly marked.

_____

4. Don't _____ your clothes by digging in that dirt!

_____

Words with /ô/

pause	strong	cause	coffee	author	daughter	often
already	taught	because	bought	applaud	gone	office
brought	caught	wrong	thought	autumn	offer	

Say and Listen

Say each spelling word. Listen for the vowel sound you hear in *pause*.

Think and Sort

Look at the letters in each word. Think about how the vowel sound in *pause* is spelled. Spell each word aloud.

The vowel sound in *pause* can be shown as /ô/. How many spelling patterns for /ô/ do you see?

autumn

1. Write the **six** spelling words that have the *au* pattern, like *pause*.
2. Write the **seven** spelling words that have the *o* pattern, like *strong*.
3. Write the **three** spelling words that have the *augh* pattern, like *taught*.
4. Write the **three** spelling words that have the *ough* pattern, like *bought*.
5. Write the **one** spelling word that has the *a* pattern.

1. au Words

_____ _____ _____

_____ _____ _____

2. o Words

_____ _____ _____

_____ _____ _____

_____

3. augh Words

_____ _____ _____

4. ough Words

_____ _____ _____

5. a Word

_____

Classifying

Write the spelling word that belongs in each group.

1. instructed, showed, _____
2. clap, cheer, _____
3. powerful, mighty, _____
4. incorrect, mistaken, _____
5. purchased, paid, _____
6. believed, supposed, _____
7. spring, summer, _____
8. captured, grabbed, _____
9. writer, creator, _____
10. stop, rest, _____
11. parent, son, _____
12. delivered, carried, _____
13. give, present, _____

If . . . Then

Write the spelling word that completes each sentence.

14. If Mary jogs four days a week, then she does it _____.
15. If Kara's cat is not here, then it is _____.
16. If Jon is finished with his work, then he's _____ done.
17. If Mom has a special room for working, then she has an

    _____.

18. If James wins many races, then it's _____ he's a fast runner.
19. If a storm can bend trees, then it might _____ them to fall.

pause	taught	wrong	author	gone
already	caught	coffee	applaud	offer
brought	cause	bought	autumn	often
strong	because	thought	daughter	office

Proofreading

Proofread the note below. Use proofreading marks to correct five spelling mistakes, three capitalization mistakes, and two punctuation mistakes.

Proofreading Marks

⬭ spell correctly

≡ capitalize

⊙ add period

August 8

Dear mr. Chang,

My mother and I went to the box ofice on main Street

and baught tickets for the play Sleeping Beauty. We want

to offer you and your daugter two of the tickets She will

enjoy the play becawse she offen reads fairy tales with

me when she comes over May i bring the tickets to

your house tomorrow afternoon?

Keisha

Titles

Underline the titles of books, plays, and movies.

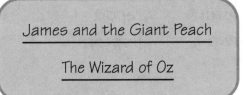

James and the Giant Peach

The Wizard of Oz

Put quotation marks around the titles of stories, poems, and songs.

"Hiawatha"   "On Top of Old Smoky"

Capitalize the first, last, and all other important words in a title.

"Take Me Out to the Ball Game"   The Other Side of the Mountain

Titles are not written correctly in the following sentences, and words are misspelled. Write each sentence correctly.

1. My favorite book, "Harry Potter and the chamber of Secrets," is gonne.

_____

_____

2. Shel Silverstein is the awthor of the poem Recipe for a Hippopotamus Sandwich.

_____

_____

3. Our music teacher tawt us the words to the song city of New Orleans.

_____

_____

More Words with /ô/

lawn	score	dawn	before	important
toward	north	crawl	shore	orbit
straw	water	quart	chorus	report
morning	explore	warm	yawn	popcorn

Say and Listen

Say each spelling word. Listen for the vowel sound you hear in *lawn*.

Think and Sort

Look at the letters in each word. Think about how the vowel sound in *lawn* is spelled. Spell each word aloud.

The vowel sound in *lawn* can be shown as /ô/. How many spelling patterns for /ô/ do you see?

popcorn

1. Write the **five** spelling words that have the *aw* pattern, like *lawn*.
2. Write the **four** spelling words that have the *a* pattern, like *water*.
3. Write the **eleven** spelling words that have the *o* pattern, like *north*.

1. aw Words

_____ _____ _____

_____ _____

2. a Words

_____ _____ _____

_____

3. o Words

_____ _____ _____

_____ _____ _____

_____ _____ _____

_____ _____

Definitions

Write the spelling word for each definition. Use a dictionary if you need to.

1. a snack food made from heating corn _____

2. ground that is covered with grass _____

3. dried stalks of grain used for padding _____

4. having great worth or value _____

5. going in the direction of something _____

6. to open the mouth and take in air when tired _____

7. the path of one heavenly body around another _____

8. the number of points made by a player or a team _____

9. organized oral or written information _____

10. the first appearance of daylight _____

Analogies

Write the spelling word that completes each analogy.

11. *Evening* is to _____ as *night* is to *day*.

12. *After* is to _____ as *up* is to *down*.

13. *South* is to _____ as *east* is to *west*.

14. *Players* are to *team* as *singers* are to _____.

15. *Find* is to *discover* as *search* is to _____.

16. *Creep* is to _____ as *walk* is to *stroll*.

17. *Dry* is to *wet* as *cool* is to _____.

18. *Pint* is to _____ as *foot* is to *yard*.

19. *Desert* is to *sand* as *lake* is to _____.

lawn	score	dawn	before	important
toward	north	crawl	shore	orbit
straw	water	quart	chorus	report
morning	explore	warm	yawn	popcorn

Proofreading

Proofread the newspaper article below. Use proofreading marks to correct five spelling mistakes, three capitalization mistakes, and two missing words.

Proofreading Marks

◯ spell correctly

≡ capitalize

∧ add

The McHenry School Report

Class Trip Big Success

One morning last week, mr. Goodkind took his students to shore along Long Beach. The bus left at doun and headed narth. The students rushed off the bus with a choras of cheers. then they ran tord the water to explore a long stretch of sandy beach. Two students had never been to the beach befour. everyone had great time.

Commas

Use a comma between the city and the state and between the day and the year.

| Tipton, Indiana | February 29, 2004 |

In a friendly letter, use a comma after the last word of the greeting and the closing.

| Dear Elliot, | Your friend, |

Add commas where they are needed in the letter below. Also, find the misspelled words and write them correctly on the lines provided.

2036 Circle Loop Drive

Richmond VA 23294

June 23 2003

Dear Donna

We're here at the lake, and it's really great. Our cabin is right on the shure. We have a view of the watter from every room.

I plan to eksplore the woods around us tomorrow morening. It has been really waurm here. The weather repourt says the rest of the week will be sunny and hot. What perfect weather for a summer vacation!

Yours truly

Dawn

1. _____ 2. _____ 3. _____

4. _____ 5. _____ 6. _____

Words with /är/ or /âr/

sharp	their	heart	stairs	stares
share	where	careful	fair	scarf
they're	smart	square	air	apart
marbles	large	there	fare	alarm

Say and Listen

The spelling words for this lesson contain the /är/ and /âr/ sounds that you hear in *sharp* and *share*. Say the spelling words. Listen for the /är/ and /âr/ sounds.

Think and Sort

Look at the letters in each word. Think about how the /är/ or /âr/ sounds are spelled. Spell each word aloud. How many spelling patterns for /är/ and /âr/ do you see?

1. The /är/ sounds can be spelled *ar* or *ear*. Write the **eight** /är/ spelling words, like *sharp*. Circle the letters that spell /är/ in each word.

2. The /âr/ sounds can be spelled *are, air, ere, eir,* or *ey're*. Write the **twelve** /âr/ spelling words, like *share*. Circle the letters that spell /âr/ in each word.

1. /är/ Words

_____   _____   _____

_____   _____   _____

_____   _____

2. /âr/ Words

_____   _____   _____

_____   _____   _____

_____   _____   _____

_____   _____   _____

Classifying

Write the spelling word that belongs in each group.

1. wind, breeze, _____

2. thorny, pointed, _____

3. bell, siren, _____

4. hat, gloves, _____

5. bright, clever, _____

6. big, huge, _____

7. separated, in pieces, _____

8. slow, watchful, _____

9. triangle, rectangle, _____

10. give, divide, _____

11. jacks, checkers, _____

12. who, what, _____

Homophones

Complete each sentence with the spelling word that is a homophone of the underlined word.

13. Steven and Jake left _____ shoes over <u>there</u>.

14. The high <u>fare</u> for the plane trip is not _____.

15. Elena <u>stares</u> at the seven flights of _____.

16. The bus _____ to the <u>fair</u> was cheap.

17. <u>They're</u> waiting over _____ by the bench.

18. Today _____ bringing <u>their</u> projects to school.

19. Jess _____ at the ball as it bounces down the <u>stairs</u>.

sharp	their	heart	stairs	stares
share	where	careful	fair	scarf
they're	smart	square	air	apart
marbles	large	there	fare	alarm

Proofreading

Proofread the directions below. Use proofreading marks to correct five spelling mistakes, three capitalization mistakes, and two unnecessary words.

Proofreading Marks

◯ spell correctly

≡ capitalize

℺ take out

How to Play Hide-and-Seek

Here's how you play hide-and-seek. first, cover

your your eyes with a skarf. Then tell everybody to

hide while you count to fifty. Be carful not to peek.

are you smeart enough to find them? Don't forget to

look under under the stairs. Remember to push larje

bushes apheart. Look until you find someone. then

that person's It and has to find someone.

Dictionary Skills

Pronunciation

A dictionary lists a pronunciation, or sound spelling, for most entry words. Special symbols are used to show the pronunciation. These symbols are listed in the pronunciation key.

stare (stâr) *v.* **stared, star·ing, stares.** To look at with a steady gaze: *Jasmine stared at the famous movie star. These sound alike:* **stare, stair.**

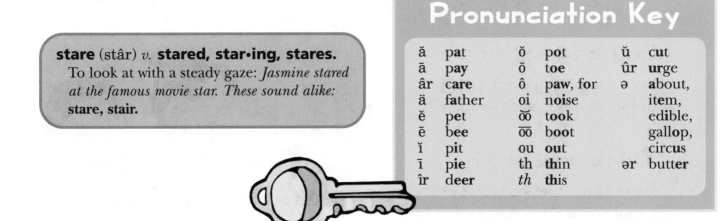

Pronunciation Key

ă	pat	ŏ	pot	ŭ	cut
ā	pay	ō	toe	ûr	urge
âr	care	ô	paw, for	ə	about,
ä	father	oi	noise		item,
ĕ	pet	ŏŏ	took		edible,
ē	bee	ōō	boot		gallop,
ĭ	pit	ou	out		circus
ī	pie	th	thin	ər	butter
îr	deer	*th*	this		

Write the correct word for each pronunciation.
Use a dictionary and the pronunciation key.

1. (wâr)   _____
2. (härt)   _____
3. (ə **lärm′**)   _____
4. (âr)   _____
5. (shärp)   _____
6. (shâr)   _____
7. (skärf)   _____
8. (smärt)   _____
9. (ə **pärt′**)   _____
10. (**mär′** bəls) _____
11. (skwâr)   _____
12. (**kâr′** fəl)   _____

Plural and Possessive Words

children	cloud's	women's	sheep	wife's
men	women	child's	oxen	knives
shelves	feet	teeth	mice	wives
man's	woman's	children's	geese	men's

Say and Listen

Say each spelling word. Listen to the sounds in each word.

children

Think and Sort

Some of the spelling words are **plural nouns.** They name more than one person, place, or thing. The usual way to form the plural of a noun is to add *-s* or *-es.* The plural nouns in this lesson are not formed in that way. They are called **irregular plurals.**

The other spelling words show ownership. They are called **possessive nouns.** How do all of these words end?

Look at each spelling word. Spell each word aloud.

1. Write the **twelve** spelling words that are plural nouns, like *men.*

2. Write the **eight** spelling words that are possessive nouns, like *man's.*

1. Plural Nouns

_____   _____   _____

_____   _____   _____

_____   _____   _____

_____   _____   _____

2. Possessive Nouns

_____   _____   _____

_____   _____   _____

_____   _____

Analogies

Write the spelling word that completes each analogy.

1. *Horses* are to *hay* as _____ are to *cheese.*

2. *Drawers* are to *dressers* as _____ are to *bookcases.*

3. *Alligators* are to *reptiles* as _____ are to *birds.*

4. *Kittens* are to *cats* as *lambs* are to _____.

5. *Lawnmowers* are to *grass* as _____ are to *food.*

6. *Fingers* are to *hands* as *toes* are to _____.

7. *Floors* are to *mop* as _____ are to *brush.*

8. *Mothers* are to *women* as *fathers* are to _____.

9. *Child* is to *children* as *ox* is to _____.

10. *Gentlemen* are to *men* as *ladies* are to _____.

11. *Ducklings* are to *ducks* as

_____ are to *humans.*

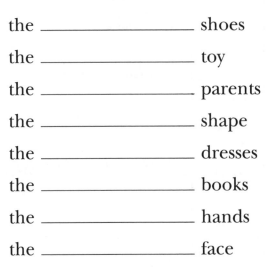

Trading Places

Write the possessive word that can be used instead of the underlined words.

12. the shoes <u>belonging to the man</u>   the _____ shoes

13. the toy <u>belonging to the child</u>   the _____ toy

14. the parents <u>of the wife</u>   the _____ parents

15. the shape <u>of the cloud</u>   the _____ shape

16. the dresses <u>belonging to the women</u>   the _____ dresses

17. the books <u>belonging to the children</u>   the _____ books

18. the hands <u>of the men</u>   the _____ hands

19. the face <u>of the woman</u>   the _____ face

children	cloud's	women's	sheep	wife's
men	women	child's	oxen	knives
shelves	feet	teeth	mice	wives
man's	woman's	children's	geese	men's

Proofreading

Proofread the list below. Use proofreading marks to correct five spelling mistakes, three capitalization mistakes, and two unnecessary words.

Proofreading Marks

◯ spell correctly

≡ capitalize

✎ take out

Things to Do

1. Polish mother's knifs, forks, and spoons.

2. Help jacob build a pen for the gooses.

3. Find a mans' suit for for the school play.

4. Wash the kitchen shelfes.

5. Write a report on sheeps for Mr. rice's class.

6. See dr. Keith to to have my teeth cleaned.

Language Connection

Possessive Nouns

An apostrophe is used to show possession, or ownership.
Add 's to a singular noun to make it possessive.

> the boy's hat = the hat that belongs to the boy
>
> the child's toy = the toy that belongs to the child

Add only an apostrophe to a plural noun that ends in s.
Add 's to a plural noun that does not end in s.

> The boys' sleds are red.   The children's sleds are fast.

Complete each sentence with the correct word from the boxes.

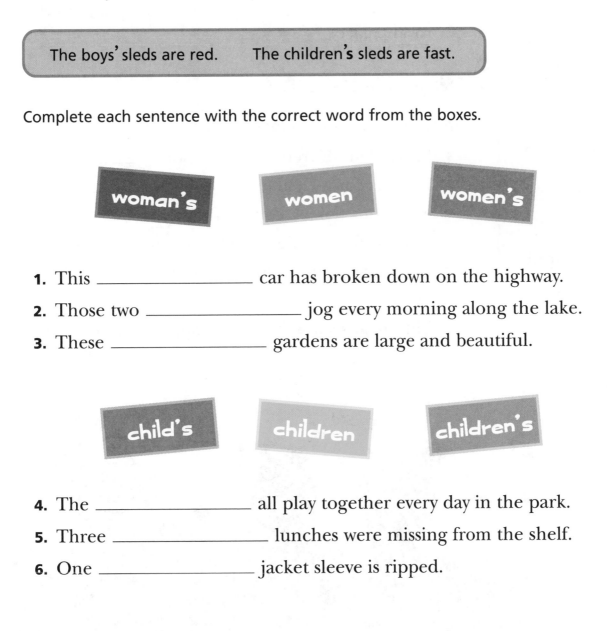

woman's   women   women's

1. This _____ car has broken down on the highway.

2. Those two _____ jog every morning along the lake.

3. These _____ gardens are large and beautiful.

child's   children   children's

4. The _____ all play together every day in the park.

5. Three _____ lunches were missing from the shelf.

6. One _____ jacket sleeve is ripped.

LESSON 21

loyal

choice

Words with /oi/

Complete each sentence by writing the spelling word that rhymes with the underlined word.

1. If you lose your <u>voice</u>, you have no _____ but to whisper.

2. The prince's _____ dog guarded the <u>royal</u> palace.

LESSON 22

autumn

daughter

wrong

often

bought

already

Words with /ô/

Write the spelling word for each clue.

3. Leaves fall off trees in this season. _____

4. If you are not right, you are this. _____

5. A parent's female child is this. _____

6. This means the same as purchased. _____

7. This means you've done something many times. _____

8. This means something has happened in the past.

_____

dawn

toward

explore

important

More Words with /ô/

Write the spelling word that completes each sentence.

9. The ocean is most beautiful at _____.

10. Kevin walked slowly _____ the frightened puppy.

11. You have an _____ decision to make.

12. Let's _____ those caves today.

marbles

heart

careful

square

stairs

where

their

they're

Words with /är/ or /âr/

Write the spelling word that completes each analogy.

13. *Dinner* is to *supper* as _____ are to *steps*.

14. *Hair* is to *hare* as *wear* is to _____.

15. *Mean* is to *cruel* as _____ is to *watchful*.

16. *Sphere* is to *circle* as *cube* is to _____.

17. *Brain* is to *think* as _____ is to *pump*.

18. *We have* is to *we've* as *they are* is to _____.

19. *Baseball* is to *sport* as _____ are to *game*.

20. *We* is to *our* as *they* is to _____.

geese

oxen

wives

wife's

men's

Plural and Possessive Words

Write the spelling word that belongs in each group.

21. ducks, swans, _____

22. husbands, children, _____

23. husband's, child's, _____

24. women's, children's, _____

25. mules, cows, _____

Words with /ûr/ or /îr/

curve	third	heard	germ	here
hear	dear	squirt	world	circle
clear	circus	early	cheer	earn
learn	skirt	birth	period	dirty

Say and Listen

The spelling words for this lesson contain the /ûr/ or /îr/ sounds that you hear in *curve* and *hear.* Say the spelling words. Listen for the /ûr/ and /îr/ sounds.

circus

Think and Sort

Look at the letters in each word. Think about how the /ûr/ or /îr/ sounds are spelled. Spell each word aloud.

How many spelling patterns for /ûr/ and /îr/ do you see?

1. Write the **fourteen** spelling words that have the /ûr/ sounds, like *curve.* Circle the letters that spell /ûr/ in each word.

2. Write the **six** spelling words that have the /îr/ sounds, like *hear.* Circle the letters that spell /îr/ in each word.

1. /ûr/ Words

_____ _____ _____

_____ _____ _____

_____ _____ _____

_____ _____ _____

_____ _____

2. /îr/ Words

_____ _____ _____

_____ _____ _____

Synonyms

Write the spelling word that is a synonym for each word.

1. bend _____

2. plain _____

3. yell _____

4. soiled _____

Analogies

Write the spelling word that completes each analogy.

5. *Continent* is to _____ as *county* is to *state.*

6. *Ending* is to *death* as *beginning* is to _____.

7. *Too* is to *two* as *deer* is to _____.

8. *Now* is to *then* as _____ is to *there.*

9. *Listened* is to _____ as *story* is to *tale.*

10. *Spend* is to _____ as *give* is to *get.*

11. *Speak* is to *mouth* as _____ is to *ear.*

12. *Door* is to *rectangle* as *plate* is to _____.

13. *Ask* is to *question mark* as *tell* is to _____.

14. *Two* is to *second* as *three* is to _____.

15. *Pour* is to *milk* as _____ is to *toothpaste.*

16. *Blouse* is to *top* as _____ is to *bottom.*

17. *School* is to _____ as *office* is to *work.*

18. *Sad* is to *happy* as *late* is to _____.

19. *Microscope* is to _____ as *telescope* is to *star.*

curve	third	heard	germ	here
hear	dear	squirt	world	circle
clear	circus	early	cheer	earn
learn	skirt	birth	period	dirty

Proofreading

Proofread the e-mail below. Use proofreading marks to correct five spelling mistakes, three capitalization mistakes, and two unnecessary words.

Proofreading Marks

◯ spell correctly

≡ capitalize

ℓ take out

---

e-mail

New	Read	File	Delete	Search	Contacts	Check

Hi, Wanda!

For my birthday Dad took me to the circas. we saw a funny clown with durty white shoes. His name was dr. Sneezo. He chased a a giant germ in a circel and tried to squert it with a bottle of green medicine. the crowd would would chear every time Dr. Sneezo tried to hit the germ. He never did it. That germ was just too fast for him. Dad and I had a great time.

Tina

Language Connection

Plurals

Plurals are words that name more than one thing. Most plurals are formed by adding -*s* or -*es* to the base word.

> To form the plural of most nouns, add -*s*.
>
> cheer + **s** = cheer**s**   circle + **s** = circle**s**
>
> If the noun ends in *s*, *x*, *ch*, *sh*, or *z*, add -*es*.
>
> fox + **es** = fox**es**   bus + **es** = bus**es**

Write the plural form of each word.

1. curve _____   **2.** birth _____

3. circus _____   **4.** brush _____

5. skirt _____   **6.** match _____

7. germ _____   **8.** box _____

9. world _____   **10.** animal _____

11. period _____   **12.** horse _____

13. circle _____   **14.** ax _____

15. branch _____   **16.** dress _____

17. cheer _____   **18.** glass _____

19. inch _____   **20.** buzz _____

Words with /ə/

together	wrinkle	summer	address	purple
animal	calendar	automobile	chapter	tickle
blizzard	special	dinosaur	whether	wander
simple	winter	Canada	whistle	United States of America

Say and Listen

Say the spelling words. Listen for the syllables that are not stressed.

automobile

Think and Sort

Most unstressed syllables have a weak vowel sound called **schwa**. It is shown as /ə/. Some words have one /ə/, and others have more than one.

Look at the letters in each word as you say each word again. Think about how /ə/ is spelled. Spell each word aloud. How many spelling patterns for /ə/ do you see?

1. Write the **fourteen** spelling words that have one /ə/ sound, like *address*. Circle the letter that spells /ə/.

2. Write the **six** spelling words that have more than one /ə/ sound, like *animal*. Circle the letters that spell /ə/.

---

1. Words with One /ə/

_____ _____ _____

_____ _____ _____

_____ _____ _____

_____ _____ _____

_____ _____

2. Words with More than One /ə/

_____ _____ _____

_____ _____ _____

Classifying

Write the spelling word that belongs in each group.

1. red, blue, _____

2. hurricane, tornado, _____

3. easy, plain, _____

4. crease, crumple, _____

5. name, _____, telephone number

6. roam, stray, _____

7. train, plane, _____

8. beast, creature, _____

Definitions

Write the spelling word for each definition. Use a dictionary if you need to.

9. at the same time _____

10. if _____

11. North American country containing fifty states _____

12. a main division of a book _____

13. the season between fall and spring _____

14. northernmost North American country _____

15. chart showing time by days, weeks, and months _____

16. not usual _____

17. the season between spring and fall _____

18. to touch lightly _____

19. to make a sound by forcing air through the lips _____

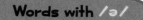

together	wrinkle	summer	address	purple
animal	calendar	automobile	chapter	tickle
blizzard	special	dinosaur	whether	wander
simple	winter	Canada	whistle	United States of America

Proofreading

Proofread the list below. Use proofreading marks to correct five spelling mistakes, three capitalization mistakes, and two unnecessary words.

Proofreading Marks

◯ spell correctly

≡ capitalize

℘ take out

Things to Do for My Art Projects

1. paint a picture of a dinosar.

2. Make lots of grass and and trees around it

   for its sumer home.

3. tape boxes tagether to make the body of a mammoth.

4. Cover the mammoth's body with strips of newspaper

   dipped in in paste.

5. glue on yarn to make its speshal covering.

6. Use white cotton balls to make the

   mammoth's wintur home.

Dictionary Skills

Accent Marks

Special symbols are often used in dictionaries to show the pronunciation of words. The schwa (ə) is a symbol for the weak vowel sound that occurs in unstressed syllables. The accent mark (′) is used to point out syllables that are spoken with more stress, or force. Some dictionaries also use dark type to show accented syllables.

Only one of the pronunciations in each pair below has the accent mark on the correct syllable. Circle the correct pronunciation and write the word. Check your answers in a dictionary.

1. /**blĭz**′ ərd/   /blĭz **ərd**′/

   _____

2. /**ăn**′əməl/   /ăn ə**məl**′/

   _____

3. /wĭs əl′/   /**wĭs**′ əl/

   _____

4. /tĭk əl′/   /**tĭk**′ əl/

   _____

5. /**sĭm**′ pəl/   /sĭm **pəl**′/

   _____

6. /**rĭng**′ kəl/   /rĭng **kəl**′/

   _____

7. /kăl ən′ dər/ /**kăl**′ən dər/

   _____

8. /**sŭm**′ ər/   /sŭm **ər**′/

   _____

9. /pûr **pəl**′/   /**pûr**′ pəl/

   _____

Compound Words

basketball	drugstore	upstairs	anything	downtown
cheeseburger	outside	inside	forever	without
countdown	everybody	nightmare	sometimes	everywhere
newspaper	birthday	afternoon	weekend	railroad

Say and Listen

Say each spelling word. Listen for the two shorter words in each word.

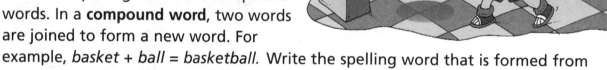

basketball

Think and Sort

All of the spelling words are compound words. In a **compound word**, two words are joined to form a new word. For example, *basket + ball = basketball.* Write the spelling word that is formed from each word pair below.

1. after + noon
2. any + thing
3. for + ever
4. some + times
5. with + out
6. every + body
7. basket + ball
8. count + down
9. in + side
10. out + side
11. night + mare
12. news + paper
13. up + stairs
14. drug + store
15. every + where
16. rail + road
17. week + end
18. birth + day
19. down + town
20. cheese + burger

1. _____
2. _____
3. _____
4. _____
5. _____
6. _____
7. _____
8. _____
9. _____
10. _____
11. _____
12. _____
13. _____
14. _____
15. _____
16. _____
17. _____
18. _____
19. _____
20. _____

Antonyms

Complete each sentence by writing the spelling word that is an antonym of the underlined word.

1. The museum is <u>uptown</u>, but the library is _____.

2. John likes eggs <u>with</u> salt but _____ pepper.

3. I went <u>downstairs</u> as Maria went _____.

4. Customers are _____, but a clerk is <u>nowhere</u> to be found.

5. We couldn't play <u>outside</u>, so we went _____.

Compound Words

Write the spelling word that can be formed by combining two words in each sentence.

6. Have you ever wished for a puppy?   _____

7. The count began with ten and went down to zero.   _____

8. We shop some of the times that we get together.   _____

9. His birth occurred on the last day of June.   _____

10. Our collie snatched the ball from the basket.   _____

11. Selma wanted cheese on her burger.   _____

12. Jill ran out and played on her side of the fence.   _____

13. We looked at every part of the frog's body.   _____

14. This unusual thing didn't come with any directions. _____

15. A rail fell off the fence and onto the road.   _____

16. The pet store sells a special drug to kill fleas.   _____

17. Most of the news in our paper is interesting.   _____

18. We eat lunch after the clock chimes at noon.   _____

19. The end of the week will be here soon.   _____

Compound Words

basketball	drugstore	upstairs	anything	downtown
cheeseburger	outside	inside	forever	without
countdown	everybody	nightmare	sometimes	everywhere
newspaper	birthday	afternoon	weekend	railroad

Proofreading

Proofread the journal entry below. Use proofreading marks to correct five spelling mistakes, two capitalization mistakes, and three punctuation mistakes.

Proofreading Marks

◯ spell correctly

≡ capitalize

⊙ add period

march 10

I went to Jo's party last weakend. There were people

everywhere. Everebody sang "Happy Birthday" to Jo Then

her mom ran upstares and brought down a large box

withowt a top What do you think Jo found inside, asleep on

some newspaper? it was a little kitten. Jo had wanted a

kitten more than anything else. I'll remember the look on her

face fourever

meow

Capital Letters

Geographic names such as names of cities, states, bodies of water, mountains, and streets are capitalized.

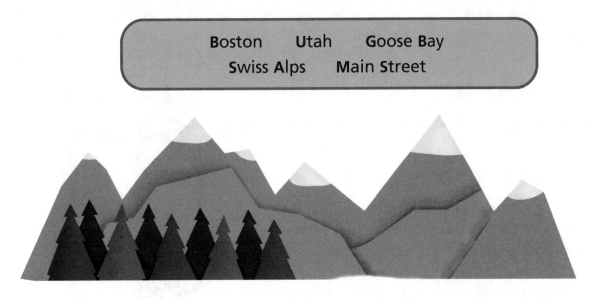

| Boston | Utah | Goose Bay |
| Swiss Alps | | Main Street |

The sentences below contain errors in capitalization and spelling. Write each sentence correctly.

1. The <u>Plain Dealer</u> is a noospaper from cleveland, ohio.

_____

2. The rialroad line was built across rollins street.

_____

3. Mr. Diaz spent the aftrnoon fishing on lake erie.

_____

4. We visited niagara falls on my burthday.

_____

5. Would you like to spend the weekind in the rocky mountains?

_____

6. Carly said she wanted to stay in carson city forevr.

_____

Abbreviations

Ave.	F	Hwy.	l	pt.
qt.	in.	gal.	mi.	C
Rd.	St.	yd.	c.	m
cm	ft.	km	Blvd.	Rte.

Say and Listen

Say the spelling word that each abbreviation stands for.

Think and Sort

All of the spelling words are abbreviations. An **abbreviation** is a shortened version of a word. Abbreviations used in street addresses and customary units of measure end with a period. Abbreviations of metric units of measurement and temperature scales do not.

1. Write the **six** abbreviations used in street addresses, like *Rte.*

2. Write the **twelve** abbreviations for units of measurement, like *qt.*

3. Write the **two** abbreviations for temperature scales, like *C.*

1. Street Addresses

_____   _____   _____

_____   _____   _____

2. Units of Measurement

_____   _____   _____

_____   _____   _____

_____   _____   _____

_____   _____   _____

3. Temperature Scales

_____   _____

Trading Places

Write the abbreviation that can be used instead of the word.

1. Fahrenheit _____
2. gallon _____
3. cup _____
4. yard _____
5. centimeter _____
6. quart _____
7. liter _____
8. Celsius _____
9. pint _____
10. mile _____
11. inch _____
12. kilometer _____
13. foot _____

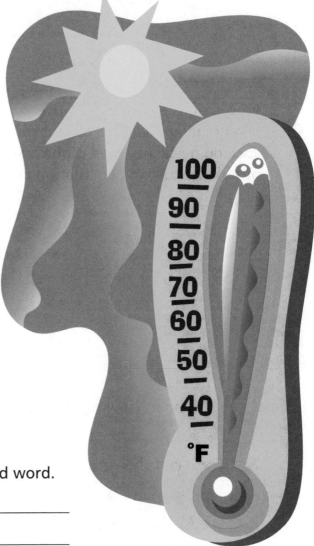

Clues

Write the spelling word for each underlined word.

14. 315 Rose <u>Boulevard</u> _____
15. <u>Route</u> 2, Box 56 _____
16. Box 1010, <u>Highway</u> 47 _____
17. 224 Main <u>Street</u> _____
18. 2067 Green <u>Road</u> _____
19. 1007 Bright <u>Avenue</u> _____

Ave.	F	Hwy.	l	pt.
qt.	in.	gal.	mi.	C
Rd.	St.	yd.	c.	m
cm	ft.	km	Blvd.	Rte.

Proofreading

Proofread the note below. Use proofreading marks to correct six spelling mistakes, three capitalization mistakes, and two punctuation mistakes.

Proofreading Marks

◯ spell correctly

≡ capitalize

⊙ add period

Kyle,

I have the key to the trunk. You can come by today after school

and get it if you want to Here are the directions to my house.

At the corner of Shady Str. and third Av., turn left and go about

50 ft down the block. go past allen Rd and turn right onto Rte. 7.

Our house is 1 mle down the road. It is white with blue trim.

The key is under a flower pot about 1 yrd from the mailbox

Ryan

End Punctuation

Three different types of punctuation can be used at the end of a sentence. The period (.) is used for a sentence that tells something or gives commands. The question mark (?) is used for a sentence that asks a question. The exclamation point (!) is used for a sentence that shows excitement or strong feeling.

I like this shirt.
Move the car, please.
Where are you going?
Our team is the greatest!

The sentences below have mistakes in end punctuation and spelling. Write each sentence correctly.

1. My family wants to follow Rt 66 on a vacation

   _____

2. Can you tell me how to get to Hway. 12

   _____

3. The temperature was 106° Fr in the shade

   _____

4. Jessica made 2 gall of lemonade

   _____

5. Our family drove 100 mil today

   _____

6. The store at 632 Rose Av belongs to my dad

   _____

Words About the Universe

rotate	Pluto	Saturn	meteor	Neptune	revolve	Mars
gravity	solar system	universe	Earth	comet	Mercury	planets
Jupiter	galaxy	Venus	satellite	Uranus	constellation	

Say and Listen

Say each spelling word. Listen for the number of syllables in each word.

solar system

Think and Sort

All of the spelling words are terms that people use to write about the universe. One of the terms is a compound word.

1. Write the **two** spelling words that have one syllable, like *Mars*.
2. Write the **eight** spelling words that have two syllables, like *Sat-urn*.
3. Write the **eight** spelling words that have three syllables, like *Ju-pi-ter*.
4. Write the **one** spelling word that has four syllables.
5. Write the **one** spelling word that is written as two words. Divide each word into syllables.

1. One-syllable Words

_____ _____

2. Two-syllable Words

_____ _____ _____

_____ _____ _____

_____ _____

3. Three-syllable Words

_____ _____ _____

_____ _____ _____

_____ _____

4. Four-syllable Word

_____

5. Compound Word

_____

Clues

Write the spelling word for each clue.

1. planet closest to the sun _____

2. seventh planet from the sun _____

3. fourth planet; the "red" one _____

4. eighth planet; named for the Roman sea god _____

5. only planet that can support animal life _____

6. second planet; named for a Roman goddess _____

7. the planet with "rings" _____

8. planet farthest from the sun _____

9. fifth planet from the sun; the largest planet _____

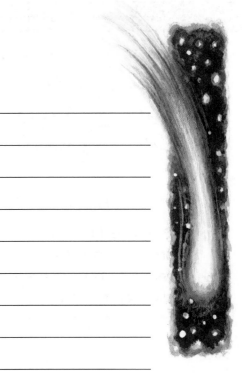

What's the Answer?

Write a spelling word that answers each question.

10. What moves around the sun and has a long tail? _____

11. What falls through space toward Earth? _____

12. What word refers to everything in space? _____

13. What names a communications object that circles Earth? _____

14. The Big Dipper is an example of what? _____

15. Mars, Jupiter, and Venus are examples of what? _____

16. What do planets do as they travel around the sun? _____

17. What keeps us from falling off Earth? _____

18. What does Earth do as it spins on its axis? _____

19. What are the sun and all the planets called as a group? _____

rotate	solar system	Venus	Neptune	Mercury
gravity	galaxy	meteor	comet	constellation
Jupiter	Saturn	Earth	Uranus	Mars
Pluto	universe	satellite	revolve	planets

Proofreading

Proofread the following paragraph from a short story. Use proofreading marks to correct five spelling mistakes, two capitalization mistakes, and three missing words.

Proofreading Marks

◯ spell correctly

☰ capitalize

∧ add

After leaving Erth, Captain diego stopped on Mercurie, venus, and Mars. He had a close call when a metiore almost hit the spaceship. When we last heard from him, he heading for Pluto, at the far edge our solor system. He plans see the whole galaxy, maybe even the uneverse.

Dictionary Skills

Using the Spelling Table

A spelling table can help you find the spelling of a word in a dictionary. Suppose you are not sure how the first vowel sound in *comet* is spelled. You can use a spelling table to find the different spellings for the sound. First, find the pronunciation symbol for the sound. Then read the first spelling listed for /ŏ/, and look up *ca* in a dictionary. Look for each spelling in a dictionary until you find the correct one.

Sound	Spellings	Examples
/ŏ/	o a	doctor, wash

Write the correct spelling for each word. Use the Spelling Table on page 141 and a dictionary.

1. klĕnz _____
2. hōst _____
3. pēch _____
4. hôrd _____
5. **lär′** və _____
6. **bûr′** glər _____
7. skwŏd _____
8. bō **kā′** _____

unit 6 Review
Lessons 26-30

Lesson 26

circle
early
world
germ
clear
here
period
cheer

Words with /ûr/ or /îr/

Write the spelling word that belongs in each group.

1. Earth, globe, _____
2. bug, virus, _____
3. beginning, first, _____
4. square, triangle, _____
5. at this place, in this spot, _____
6. shout, yell, _____
7. comma, hyphen, _____
8. obvious, plain, _____

Lesson 27

whether
special
automobile
animal
wrinkle

Words with /ə/

Write the spelling word that completes each analogy.

9. *Drive* is to _____ as *fly* is to *plane*.
10. *Though* is to *however* as _____ is to *if*.
11. *Garden* is to *flower* as *zoo* is to _____.
12. *Crease* is to _____ as *flat* is to *level*.
13. *Unique* is to *common* as _____ is to *ordinary*.

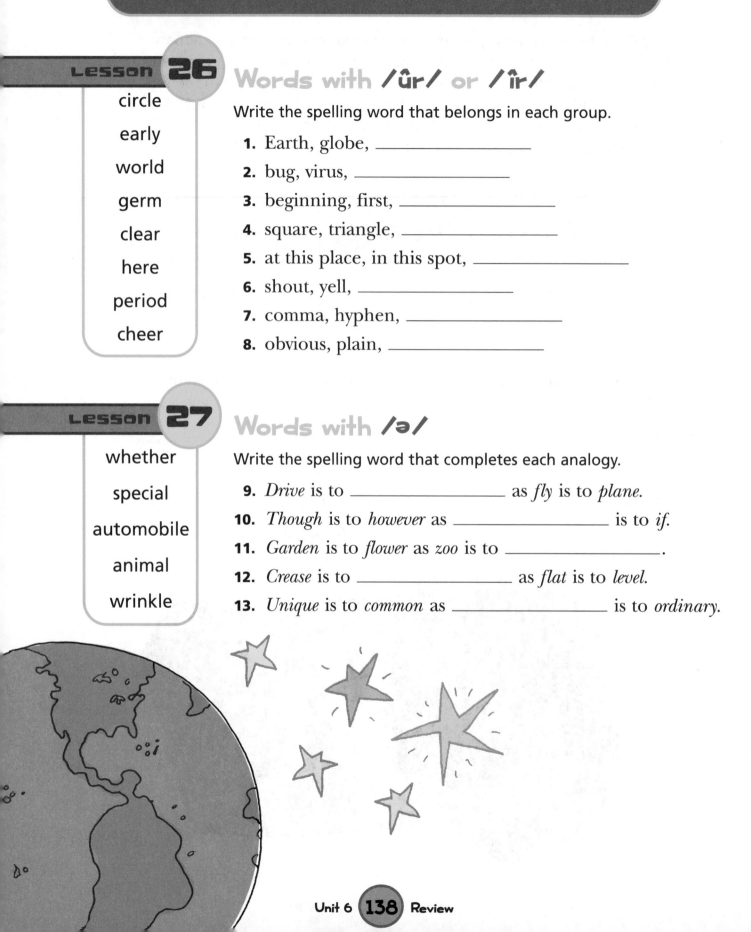

LESSON 28

without

everywhere

birthday

Compound Words

Write the spelling word that completes each sentence.

14. If you don't have any assignments, you are _____ homework.

15. When something is in all places, it is _____.

16. When you become a year older, you celebrate your _____.

LESSON 29

Blvd.

in.

gal.

cm

F

Abbreviations

Write the spelling word that is the abbreviation for the underlined word in each phrase.

17. 12 <u>inches</u> _____

18. 98° <u>Fahrenheit</u> _____

19. 631 River <u>Boulevard</u> _____

20. 3 <u>gallons</u> _____

21. 5 <u>centimeters</u> _____

LESSON 30

Mercury

satellite

gravity

constellation

Words About the Universe

Write the spelling word for each definition.

22. a heavenly body that revolves around a planet

_____

23. the force that causes objects to move toward the center of the Earth _____

24. the planet closest to the sun _____

25. a group of stars with a recognizable shape

_____

commonly misspelled words

about	every	myself	they
above	family	name	they're
across	favorite	nice	though
again	finally	now	through
a lot	first	once	today
always	friend	other	together
another	get	outside	tomorrow
beautiful	getting	party	too
because	goes	people	two
been	guess	play	until
before	happened	please	upon
beginning	have	pretty	very
believe	hear	read	want
birthday	here	really	went
bought	hospital	right	were
buy	house	said	we're
came	into	saw	when
children	it's	scared	where
come	know	school	with
cousin	little	sent	would
didn't	made	some	write
different	make	sometimes	writing
does	many	swimming	wrote
doesn't	might	their	your
enough	morning	there	you're

spelling table

Sound	Spellings	Examples
/ă/	a ai au	match, plaid, laugh
/ā/	a a_e ai ay ea ei eigh ey	April, chase, plain, day, break, reign, eight, obey
/ä/	a	father
/âr/	air are eir ere ey're	fair, share, their, there, they're
/b/	b bb	bus, rabbit
/ch/	ch tch t	child, match, picture
/d/	d dd	dish, address
/ĕ/	e ea ie ai ue	never, bread, friend, again, guess
/ē/	e e_e ea ee ei eo ey i i_e ie y	zebra, these, please, sweet, deceive, people, key, ski, police, cities, city
/f/	f ff gh	feet, offer, laugh
/g/	g gg	go, jogging
/h/	h wh	hope, who
/ĭ/	i a e ee u ui y	quick, package, secret, been, busy, building, gym
/ī/	i i_e ie igh eye uy y	child, life, die, night, eyesight, buy, dry
/îr/	er ear eer eir ere	period, hear, cheer, weird, here
/j/	j g dg	jog, tragic, edge
/k/	k c ck ch	keep, coast, package, chorus
/ks/	x	axle
/kw/	qu	squeeze
/l/	l ll	life, balloon
/m/	m mb mm	man, comb, swimming

Sound	Spellings	Examples
/n/	n kn nn	nose, knot, beginning
/ng/	n ng	monkey, anything
/ŏ/	o a	doctor, wash
/ō/	o o_e oa oe ow ou ough	zero, those, coach, toe, hollow, boulder, though
/oi/	oi oy	coin, royal
/ô/	o a au augh aw ough	strong, already, cause, taught, shawl, bought
/ŏŏ/	oo o ou u	wool, wolf, could, full
/ōō/	oo ew u u_e ue ui o ou	shoot, grew, truly, tune, blue, fruit, two, soup
/ou/	ou ow	ours, towel
/p/	p pp	pay, happen
/r/	r rr wr	reply, hurry, wrinkle
/s/	s ss c	save, pass, fence
/sh/	sh s ce	shape, sugar, ocean
/t/	t tt ed	taste, button, thanked
/th/	th	that
/th/	th	thick
/ŭ/	u o o_e oe oo ou	brush, month, become, does, blood, touch
/ûr/	ur ir er ear ere or our	curve, third, germ, earn, were, world, flourish
/v/	v f	voice, of
/w/	w wh o	win, where, once
/y/	y	yawn
/yōō/	u_e ew eau	use, new, beautiful
/z/	z zz s	zebra, blizzard, trees
/ə/	a e i o u	special, often, family, together, surprise

Answer Key

Page 8
1. past, match, ask, snack, stamp, magic, pass, happen, answer, travel, plastic, grass, began, crack, glad, branch, half, banana
2. laugh, aunt

Page 9
1. crack
2. happen
3. magic
4. travel
5. stamp
6. grass
7. plastic
8. began
9. glad
10. half
11. answer
12. snack
13. banana
14. branch
15. laugh
16. aunt
17. past
18. ask
19. pass

Page 10
Spell correctly: crack, travel, branch, happen, pass
Add period after: thunder, shore, quickly
Add: the [between "Watch" and "sky"]; a [between "hear" and "loud"]

Page 11
1. glad, laugh, stamp
2. grass, magic, plastic
3. banana, began, brick
4. answer, ask, aunt
5. half, happy, have
6. crack, crisp, crumb

Page 12
1. awake, chase, mistake, trade, waste, taste, plane, space, state, shape
2. paid, plain, afraid, trail, wait, waist
3. eight, eight, neighbor
4. break

Page 13
1. plain
2. plane
3. waste
4. waist
5. weight
6. wait
7. taste
8. chase
9. trade
10. trail
11. state
12. space
13. paid
14. shape
15. eight
16. break
17. mistake
18. afraid
19. awake

Page 14
Spell correctly: state, trail, Taste, space, mistake
Capitalize: Are, See, It
Take out: to, be

Page 15
1. chase
2. awake
3. trade
4. railroad
5. rotate
6. shape
7. trail
8. lightweight
9. acquaint
10. betray
11. save

Page 16
1. edge, ever, never, echo, energy, fence, stretch, yesterday, desert
2. bread, ready, heavy, health, breakfast, weather, sweater
3. again, against
4. friend
5. guess

Page 17
1. desert
2. health
3. friend
4. guess
5. heavy
6. never
7. edge
8. against
9. yesterday
10. ready
11. again
12. ever
13. weather
14. bread
15. sweater
16. fence
17. stretch
18. echo
19. energy

Page 18
Spell correctly: Yesterday, friend, weather, breakfast, energy
Capitalize: July, We, Maria
Add: with [between "tennis" and "my"]; the/our [between "start" and "day"]

Page 19
1. again, age
2. sweater, stretch
3. health, heavy

Page 20
1. season, scream, reason, beach, teach, means, speak, leaf, treat, peace, please
2. knee, queen, between, sweep, sweet, speech, seem, freeze, squeeze

Page 21
1. sweep
2. queen
3. leaf
4. knee
5. scream
6. between
7. sweet
8. means
9. please
10. season
11. treat
12. speak
13. seem
14. speech
15. beach
16. squeeze
17. reason
18. freeze
19. peace

Page 22
Spell correctly: teach, means, season, freeze, reason
Add question mark after: team, spring, again
Add: of [between "member" and "a"]; the [between "of" and "year"]

Page 23
1. sweep
2. seem
3. scream
4. means
5. speak
6. squeeze

Page 24
1. March, May, June
2. Friday, Thursday, July, August, Sunday, Monday, Tuesday, Wednesday, April
3. October, December, September, November, Saturday
4. February, January
5. Dr.

Page 25
1. February
2. Sunday
3. Tuesday
4. December
5. September
6. Saturday
7. November
8. Wednesday
9. April
10. Monday
11. October
12. Thursday
13. August
14. Dr.
15. May
16. June
17. March
18. July
19. Friday

Page 26
Spell correctly: Dr., Monday, Tuesday, Friday, February
Capitalize: Wilson, Saturday, Eric's
Take out: to, the

Page 27
1. Jan-u-ar-y
2. Feb-ru-ar-y
3. A-pril
4. Ju-ly
5. Au-gust
6. Sep-tem-ber
7. No-vem-ber
8. De-cem-ber
9. Mon-day
10. Wednes-day
11. Thurs-day
12. Fri-day
13. Sat-ur-day

Page 28
1. answer
2. travel
3. aunt
4. half
5. laugh
6. afraid
7. eight
8. mistake
9. taste
10. neighbor
11. break

Page 29
12. friend
13. stretch
14. against
15. energy
16. sweater
17. guess
18. reason
19. please
20. knee
21. speech
22. January
23. February
24. Wednesday
25. Dr.

Page 30
1. zebra, secret
2. easy, every, body, family, copy, busy, city, angry, plenty, hungry, sorry
3. radio, piano, ski, pizza
4. evening
5. people
6. police

Page 31
1. radio
2. secret
3. police
4. sorry
5. busy
6. ski
7. pizza
8. zebra
9. copy
10. city
11. body
12. easy
13. every
14. angry
15. evening
16. people
17. plenty
18. family
19. hungry

Page 32
Spell correctly: Family, easy, every, people, busy
Capitalize: Saturday, Harvey, Follow
Take out: is, we

Page 33
1. I told the secret to Amy, Will, and Edward.
2. I love music so much that I play the violin, the piano, and the flute.
3. At the zoo we saw a zebra, an elephant, and a lion.
4. I like pizza with cheese, peppers, and onions.
5. Everyone in my family likes to ski, skate, and sled.
6. The busy city has plenty of people, cars, and buses.
7. Rita, Jenna, Karen, and Kim play soccer.

Page 34
1. village, package
2. gym
3. quick, deliver, different, picture, middle, interesting, written, bridge, thick, picnic, inch, begin, pitch, itch, chicken
4. guitar, building

Page 35
1. pitch
2. different
3. begin
4. quick
5. thick
6. interesting
7. written
8. deliver
9. chicken
10. inch
11. bridge
12. middle
13. picture
14. village
15. guitar
16. package
17. itch
18. building
19. gym

Page 36
Spell correctly: thick, village, middle, building, quick
Capitalize: People, Firefighters, It's
Add question mark after: go, return

Page 37
1. 2
2. 1
3. 3
4. gui-tar
5. pic-ture
6. pic-nic
7. writ-ten
8. be-gin
9. pack-age
10. dif-fer-ent
11. build-ing

Page 38
1. night, mighty, fight, flight, right, might, midnight, tonight, lightning, highway, high, bright, sight
2. dry, spy, supply, reply, deny
3. tie, die

Page 39
1. bright
2. right
3. mighty
4. night
5. lightning
6. high
7. sight
8. reply
9. deny
10. dry
11. midnight
12. tie
13. might
14. flight
15. fight
16. die
17. tonight
18. supply
19. spy

Page 40
Spell correctly: supply, night, midnight, spy, reply
Capitalize: Jessica, September, August
Take out: a, by

Page 41
1. 2
2. 1
3. 1
4. 2
5. 1
6. 2
7. 3
8. 1
9. 2
10. 3
11. 3

Page 42
1. life, knife, awhile, sunshine, smile, slide, beside, twice, write, surprise, size, wise
2. quiet, giant, climb, blind, behind, child, iron
3. buy

Page 43
1. surprise
2. giant
3. sunshine
4. behind
5. quiet
6. beside
7. iron
8. awhile
9. knife
10. smile
11. size
12. twice
13. life
14. buy
15. child
16. slide
17. climb
18. wise
19. blind

Page 44
Spell correctly: life, quiet, surprise, wise, climb
Add period after: tail, off, though
Take out: and, a

Page 45
1. giant
2. knife
3. iron
4. joy
5. smile
6. child
7. sunshine
8. size

Page 46
1. brothers, trees, pockets, rocks, hikes, gloves
2. dishes, classes, buses, brushes, inches, branches, peaches, foxes, boxes
3. families, pennies, cities, babies, stories

Page 47
1. buses
2. cities
3. rocks
4. brothers
5. pennies
6. boxes
7. inches
8. foxes
9. branches
10. babies
11. stories
12. families
13. trees
14. pockets
15. hikes
16. gloves
17. dishes
18. classes
19. brushes

Page 48
Spell correctly: families, cities, hikes, rocks, babies
Add period after: woods, watch, wildlife
Add: to [between "rocks" and "climb"]; as [between "such" and "rabbits"]

Page 49
1. Peaches
2. Her older brothers
3. Two cardboard boxes
4. Dance classes
5. My aunt's twin babies
6. The oak trees

Page 50
1. family
2. secret
3. radio
4. evening
5. people
6. police
7. gym
8. building
9. different
10. package
11. interesting
12. picture

Page 51
13. lightning
14. tie
15. tonight
16. supply
17. quiet
18. buy
19. climb
20. surprise
21. pennies
22. babies
23. inches
24. brothers
25. families

Page 52
1. hobby, model, forgot, doctor, contest, object, o'clock, cotton, dollar, solve, knock, problem, bottom, beyond, knot, hospital
2. wash, wallet, watch, swallow

Page 53
1. swallow
2. knock
3. wash
4. watch
5. dollar
6. solve
7. cotton
8. contest
9. object
10. wallet
11. model
12. beyond
13. doctor
14. forgot
15. o'clock
16. knot
17. bottom
18. hobby
19. problem

Page 54
Spell correctly: hobby, wallet, watch, bottom, o'clock
Capitalize: Enter, Friday, Anyone
Add period after: page, enter

Page 55
1. beyond, preposition
2. cotton, noun
3. dollar, noun
4. forgot, verb
5. hospital, noun
6. knock, verb or noun
7. problem, noun

Page 56
1. clothes, total, ocean, obey, pony, poem, almost, only, comb, motor, hotel, zero, program
2. oak, throat, coach, coast, soap
3. goes, toe

Page 57
1. coast
2. almost
3. obey
4. total
5. goes
6. ocean
7. only
8. program
9. soap
10. zero
11. hotel
12. pony
13. comb
14. throat
15. poem
16. toe
17. oak
18. coach
19. clothes

Page 58
Spell correctly: coast, hotel, toe, comb, almost
Capitalize: August, Our, I
Take out: to, the

Page 59
1. Laurie, Amber, and Keisha climbed to the top of the rope.
2. Miss Santucci said that the ropes feel as if they've been coated with soap.
3. On Tuesday we have basketball practice with Mr. Dowling.
4. Rebecca and Jamal keep track of the points that each team scores.

Page 60
1. froze, alone, broke, explode, chose, close, nose, those, stole
2. below, elbow, knows, pillow, own, hollow, shadow, slowly, tomorrow, window
3. though

Page 61
1. hollow
2. broke
3. close
4. slowly
5. froze
6. below
7. alone
8. stole
9. pillow
10. elbow
11. chose
12. tomorrow
13. nose
14. knows
15. explode
16. shadow
17. own
18. those
19. though

Page 62
Spell correctly: froze, window, though, shadow, slowly
Capitalize: Suddenly, Then, Who
Add question mark after: window, night

Page 63
1. Bob said, "The door to the cellar door froze shut."
2. "My model car broke!" yelled Michael.
3. "Is something living in that hollow log?" asked Delia.
4. Zak yelled, "Look at your shadow on the wall!"
5. "Stay close together as we hike," said the guide.
6. Randi asked, "Is this pillow made of feathers?"

Page 64
1. suddenly, knuckle, brush, button, fudge, hunt, until, subject, under, jungle, hundred
2. rough, trouble, touch, couple, enough, tough, country, double
3. does

Page 65
1. brush
2. rough
3. fudge
4. knuckle
5. double
6. tough
7. under
8. does
9. subject
10. until
11. country
12. hundred
13. couple
14. trouble
15. touch
16. suddenly
17. enough
18. jungle

Page 66
Spell correctly: tough, until, country, trouble, enough
Capitalize: Friday, Luther, Dr.
Add question mark after: week, about

Page 67
1. couple, kŭp′ əl
2. hundred, hŭn′ drĭd
3. rough, rŭf
4. touch, tŭch
5. tough
6. country
7. knuckle
8. subject
9. suddenly
10. enough

Page 68
1. weren't, doesn't, isn't, wouldn't, wasn't, aren't, don't, hadn't, haven't, didn't, shouldn't, couldn't
2. a. I'm
b. that's
c. we're
d. let's
e. they've
f. you'd
g. she'd
h. they'll

Page 69
1. I'm
2. they've
3. she'd
4. we're
5. you'd
6. let's
7. they'll
8. that's
9. weren't
10. didn't
11. don't
12. doesn't
13. wasn't
14. haven't
15. wouldn't
16. shouldn't
17. isn't
18. aren't
19. hadn't

Page 70
Spell correctly: didn't, couldn't, weren't, I'm, that's
Capitalize: He, Bill, I
Add period after: nap, any

Page 71
1. The video store didn't have the movie I wanted.
2. We're starting a computer club at school.
3. Becca doesn't want the lead role in the play.
4. You'd better pack your long raincoat.
5. The guide said she'd meet us by the iron gate.

Page 72
1. dollar
2. doctor
3. problem
4. watch
5. swallow
6. knock
7. hospital
8. goes
9. clothes
10. poem
11. throat
12. ocean

Page 73
13. froze
14. though
15. knows
16. tomorrow
17. suddenly
18. tough
19. does
20. jungle
21. trouble
22. doesn't
23. we're
24. they've
25. weren't

Page 74
1. wonderful, discover, among, front, other, brother, money, cover, month, monkey, sponge, nothing, stomach, once, another, won
2. done, above, become
3. blood

Page 75
1. above
2. front
3. done
4. won
5. wonderful
6. nothing
7. brother
8. stomach
9. once
10. become
11. blood
12. sponge
13. month
14. among
15. monkey
16. other
17. money
18. another
19. cover

Page 76
Spell correctly: once, Another, stomach, become, wonderful
Add period after: Zoo, stomach, doctor
Take out: what, he

Page 77
1. underline second pronunciation; money
2. underline second pronunciation; nothing
3. underline first pronunciation; brother
4. yes
5. da
6. yesterday
7. noon
8. af
9. afternoon

Page 78
1. wool, understood, cooked, stood, notebook, brook, wooden, good-bye
2. full, bush, sugar, pull, pudding, during
3. should, could, would, yours
4. wolf, woman

Page 79
1. pull
2. woman
3. during
4. brook
5. full
6. bush
7. wool
8. pudding
9. sugar
10. cooked
11. notebook
12. wolf
13. yours
14. stood
15. wooden
16. could
17. should
18. would
19. understood

Page 80
Spell correctly: woman, during, brook, sugar, wool
Capitalize: Lee, On, Lee's
Add period after: farm, time

Page 81
1. My father could not fix our broken lawnmower.
2. Uncle Frank and Dad stood in line for baseball tickets.
3. Danny's father said good-bye to Dr. Dominguez.
4. We took a picture of Mom and Dad near the wooden bridge.
5. My aunt asked Uncle Mike to share his recipe for bread pudding.

Page 82
1. goose, balloon, too, cartoon, loose, shoot, choose
2. knew, grew, new
3. truly, truth
4. cougar, route, soup, group, through
5. fruit, two, beautiful

Page 83
1. shoot
2. new
3. route
4. through
5. too
6. knew
7. two
8. beautiful
9. truth
10. group
11. balloon
12. loose
13. goose
14. fruit
15. truly
16. soup
17. cartoon
18. choose
19. grew

Page 84
Spell correctly: goose, truth, beautiful, group, new
Capitalize: The, Canada, Sometimes
Add period after: America, parks

Page 85
1. new
2. knew
3. two
4. too
5. new, knew
6. two, too

Page 86
1. loud, counter, hours, sour, cloud, ours, south, mouth, noun, proud
2. somehow, crowd, growl, towel, crowded, vowel, shower, crown, tower

Page 87
1. crown
2. hours
3. mouth
4. crowd
5. sour
6. loud
7. shower
8. growl
9. south
10. powerful
11. ours
12. crowded
13. counter
14. somehow
15. tower
16. towel
17. cloud
18. proud
19. vowel

Page 88
Spell correctly: vowel, noun, somehow, powerful, proud
Capitalize: October, A, I
Add: is [between "writing" and "amazing"]; are [between "words" and "put"]

Page 89
1. Julie said, "A big crowd always comes to see our team play."
2. "They practice for three hours each day," said Brian.
3. "Even when they're behind, they don't throw in the towel," said Chris.
4. "Let's give them a loud cheer!" shouted Ben.

Page 90
1. asked, trying, carrying
2. hoping, changed, pleased, caused, traded, closing, invited, tasted, saving, writing
3. swimming, beginning, jogging
4. studied, copied, dried, cried

Page 91
1. carrying
2. swimming
3. jogging
4. tasted
5. writing
6. cried
7. studied
8. traded
9. saving
10. hoping
11. closing
12. asked
13. pleased
14. copied
15. invited
16. beginning
17. dried
18. changed
19. caused

Page 92
Spell correctly: jogging, studied, cried, Saving, pleased
Capitalize: Street, Meanwhile, Theo
Take out: could, had

Page 93
1. invited me to come to her house last summer
2. swam in the pool each day
3. traded our favorite mystery stories
4. is writing a book
5. are reading her other books

Page 94
1. discover
2. blood
3. wonderful
4. stomach
5. once
6. sugar
7. should
8. understood
9. woman
10. during
11. through
12. beautiful
13. two
14. loose
15. truly

Page 95
16. fruit
17. knew
18. crowd
19. loud
20. ours
21. asked
22. trying
23. beginning
24. copied
25. hoping

Page 96
1. enjoy, destroy, employ, employer, loyal, royal, voyage, loyalty, soybean
2. coin, moisture, spoil, point, poison, soil, join, avoid, voice, noise, choice

Page 97
1. voyage
2. poison
3. soil
4. loyal
5. choice
6. coin
7. point
8. voice
9. employer
10. soybean
11. loyalty
12. moisture
13. destroy
14. join
15. spoil
16. enjoy
17. noise
18. employ
19. avoid

Page 98
Spell correctly: enjoy, spoil, destroy, moisture, soil
Add period after: year, crop, too
Take out: this, can

Page 99
1. soil, noun
2. poison, verb
3. poison, noun
4. soil, verb

Page 100
1. pause, cause, because, author, applaud, autumn
2. strong, wrong, coffee, gone, offer, often, office
3. taught, caught, daughter
4. brought, bought, thought
5. already

Page 101
1. taught
2. applaud
3. strong
4. wrong
5. bought
6. thought
7. autumn
8. caught
9. author
10. pause
11. daughter
12. brought
13. offer
14. often
15. gone
16. office
17. office
18. because
19. cause

Page 102
Spell correctly: office, bought, daughter, because, often
Capitalize: Mr., Main, I
Add period after: tickets, over

Page 103
1. My favorite book, _Harry Potter and the Chamber of Secrets_, is gone.
2. Shel Silverstein is the author of the poem "Recipe for a Hippopotamus Sandwich."
3. Our music teacher taught us the words to the song "City of New Orleans."

143

Page 104
1. lawn, straw, dawn, crawl, yawn
2. toward, water, quart, warm
3. morning, score, north, explore, before, shore, chorus, important, orbit, report, popcorn

Page 105
1. popcorn
2. lawn
3. straw
4. important
5. toward
6. yawn
7. orbit
8. score
9. report
10. dawn
11. morning
12. before
13. north
14. chorus
15. explore
16. crawl
17. warm
18. quart
19. water

Page 106
Spell correctly: dawn, north, chorus, toward, before
Capitalize: Mr., Then, Everyone
Add: the [between "to" and "shore"]; a [between "had" and "great"]

Page 107
Add comma after: Richmond, 23, Donna, truly
1. shore
2. water
3. explore
4. morning
5. warm
6. report

Page 108
1. sharp, marbles, smart, large, heart, scarf, apart, alarm,
2. share, they're, their, where, careful, square, there, stairs, fair, air, fare, stares

Page 109
1. air
2. sharp
3. alarm
4. scarf
5. smart
6. large
7. apart
8. careful
9. square
10. share
11. marbles
12. where
13. their
14. fair
15. stairs
16. fare
17. there
18. they're
19. stares

Page 110
Spell correctly: scarf, careful, smart, large, apart
Capitalize: First, Are, Then
Take out: your, under

Page 111
1. where
2. heart
3. alarm
4. air
5. sharp
6. share
7. scarf
8. smart
9. apart
10. marbles
11. square
12. careful

Page 112
1. children, men, shelves, women, feet, teeth, sheep, oxen, mice, geese, knives, wives

2. man's, cloud's, woman's, women's, child's, children's, wife's, men's

Page 113
1. mice
2. shelves
3. geese
4. sheep
5. knives
6. feet
7. teeth
8. men
9. oxen
10. women
11. children
12. man's
13. child's
14. wife's
15. cloud's
16. women's
17. children's
18. men's
19. woman's

Page 114
Spell correctly: knives, geese, man's, shelves, sheep
Capitalize: Jacob, Rice's, Dr.
Take out: for, to

Page 115
1. woman's
2. women
3. women's
4. children
5. children's
6. child's

Page 116
1. choice
2. loyal
3. autumn
4. wrong
5. daughter
6. bought
7. often
8. already

Page 117
9. dawn
10. toward
11. important
12. explore
13. stairs
14. where
15. careful
16. square
17. heart
18. they're
19. marbles
20. their
21. geese
22. wives
23. wife's
24. men's
25. oxen

Page 118
1. curve, learn, third, circus, skirt, heard, squirt, early, birth, germ world, circle, earn, dirty
2. hear, clean, dear, cheer, period, here

Page 119
1. curve
2. clear
3. cheer
4. dirty
5. world
6. birth
7. dear
8. here
9. heard
10. earn
11. hear
12. circle
13. period
14. third
15. squirt
16. skirt
17. learn
18. early
19. germ

Page 120
Spell correctly: circus, dirty, circle, squirt, cheer
Capitalize: We, Dr. The
Take out: a, would

Page 121
1. curves
2. births
3. circuses
4. brushes
5. skirts
6. matches
7. germs
8. boxes
9. worlds
10. animals
11. periods
12. horses
13. circles
14. axes
15. branches
16. dresses
17. cheers
18. glasses
19. inches
20. buzzes

Page 122
1. blizzard, simple, wrinkle, special, winter, summer, dinosaur, address, chapter, whether, whistle purple, tickle, wander
2. together, animal, calendar, automobile, Canada, United States of America

Page 123
1. purple
2. blizzard
3. simple
4. wrinkle
5. address
6. wander
7. automobile
8. animal
9. together
10. whether
11. United States of America
12. chapter
13. winter
14. Canada
15. calendar
16. special
17. summer
18. tickle
19. whistle

Page 124
Spell correctly: dinosaur, summer, together, special, winter
Capitalize: Paint, Tape, Glue
Take out: and, in

Page 125
1. circle first pronunciation, blizzard
2. circle first pronunciation, animal
3. circle second pronunciation, whistle
4. circle second pronunciation, tickle
5. circle first pronunciation, simple
6. circle first pronunciation, wrinkle
7. circle second pronunciation, calendar
8. circle first pronunciation, summer
9. circle second pronunciation, purple

Page 126
1. afternoon
2. anything
3. forever
4. sometimes
5. without
6. everybody
7. basketball
8. countdown
9. inside
10. outside
11. nightmare
12. newspaper
13. upstairs
14. drugstore
15. everywhere
16. railroad
17. weekend
18. birthday
19. downtown
20. cheeseburger

Page 127
1. downtown
2. without
3. upstairs
4. everywhere
5. inside
6. forever
7. countdown
8. sometimes
9. birthday
10. basketball
11. cheeseburger
12. outside
13. everybody
14. anything
15. railroad
16. drugstore
17. newspaper
18. afternoon
19. weekend

Page 128
Spell correctly: weekend, Everybody, upstairs, without, forever
Capitalize: March, It
Add period after: Jo, top, forever

Page 129
1. The Plain Dealer is a newspaper from Cleveland, Ohio.
2. The railroad line was built across Rollins Street.
3. Mr. Diaz spent the afternoon fishing on Lake Erie.
4. Would you like to spend the weekend in the Rocky Mountains?

5. Carly said she wanted to stay in Carson City forever.

Page 130
1. Ave., Rd., St., Hwy., Blvd., Rte.
2. qt., cm, in., ft., gal., yd., km, l, mi., c., pt., m
3. F, C

Page 131
1. F
2. gal.
3. c.
4. yd.
5. cm
6. qt.
7. l
8. C
9. pt.
10. mi.
11. in.
12. km
13. ft.
14. Blvd.
15. Rte.
16. Hwy.
17. St.
18. Rd.
19. Ave.

Page 132
Spell correctly: St., Ave., ft., Rd., mi., yd.
Capitalize: Third, Go, Allen
Add period after: to, mailbox

Page 133
1. My family wants to follow Rte. 66 on a vacation.
2. Can you tell me how to get to Hwy. 12?
3. The temperature was 106° F in the shade!
4. Jessica made 2 gal. of lemonade.
5. Our family drove 100 mi. today.
6. The store at 632 Rose Ave. belongs to my dad.

Page 134
1. Earth, Mars
2. rotate, Pluto, Saturn, Venus, Neptune, comet, revolve, planets
3. gravity, Jupiter, galaxy, universe, meteor, satellite, Uranus, Mercury
4. constellation
5. so-lar sys-tem

Page 135
1. Mercury
2. Uranus
3. Mars
4. Neptune
5. Earth
6. Venus
7. Saturn
8. Pluto
9. Jupiter
10. comet
11. meteor
12. universe
13. satellite
14. constellation
15. planets
16. revolve
17. gravity
18. rotate
19. solar system

Page 136
Spell correctly: Earth, Mercury, meteor, solar, universe
Capitalize: Diego, Venus
Add: was [between "he" and "heading"], of [between "edge" and "our"], to [between "plans" and "see"]

Page 137
1. cleanse
2. host
3. peach
4. hoard
5. larva
6. burglar
7. squad
8. bouquet

Page 138
1. world
2. germ
3. early
4. circle
5. here
6. cheer
7. period
8. clear
9. automobile
10. whether
11. animal
12. wrinkle
13. special

Page 139
14. without
15. everywhere
16. birthday
17. in.
18. F
19. Blvd.
20. gal.
21. cm
22. satellite
23. gravity
24. Mercury
25. constellation